THE
WHISKEY ROW
FIRE OF 1900

THE
WHISKEY ROW
FIRE of 1900

Thank you for visiting the Palace and Whiskey Row!

Bradley G. Courtney

BRADLEY G. COURTNEY

WITH CONTRIBUTION BY MARSHALL TRIMBLE, ARIZONA STATE HISTORIAN

THE
History
PRESS

Published by The History Press
Charleston, SC
www.historypress.com

First published 2020

Manufactured in the United States

ISBN 9781467143158

Library of Congress Control Number: 2019951264

This book is dedicated to the memory of Holly Joy Courtney, the great love of my life. Your middle name is absolutely appropriate, for you brought it to everyone who knew you. You were truly gioia *for us all.*

CONTENTS

FOREWORD

Fires were always a menace to frontier towns. The first generation of these communities, especially the business districts, were usually made of wood. With all those coal oil lamps, stoves and lighted candles, it took only one careless mistake, and it was Katie bar the door. The whole town would go up in smoke. The boomtowns of Prescott, Bisbee, Jerome and Tombstone all burned to the ground, sometimes more than once during their early years.

Immediately after the ashes cooled, those hardy, determined citizens were out digging through the debris to salvage what they could use again. After each fire, they rebuilt with less lumber and more brick and mortar.

I love the story told of the morning after Prescott's Great Fire, when the businessmen and women were salvaging what they could from the ruins and opening up for business on the sidewalk. No one was demanding the federal government come in and take care of them. Not these plucky folks. They were not going to stand around wringing their hands in despair— they had work to do. They were going to rebuild their community and make it even better than the one before. And they did.

I have always been a serious historian with great respect for the facts. I also work the "beef and beans" circuit as a speaker who loves to share the colorful history of Arizona. I have been at it long enough to know stories tend to become embellished with each telling. My audiences are nearly always folks with a love of Arizona and the West. And they like a good story. Sometimes I find myself questioning the veracity of a story that I have been telling for years.

I have stopped counting the times I have had to do some fact-checking and have had to change my introduction to say, "There's a possibility this one will take you down the path of plausibility, and you're going to have to figure out where to get off." I think it was Mark Twain who said, "If it didn't happen this way, it coulda happened this way." Or maybe he said, "shoulda happened this way."

That is supposed to get me off the hook in case some scholar comes forth and confronts me with some new research disproving my time-honored story.

That being said, I will leave it to my friend Brad Courtney to reveal the whole story of the Great Fire. In his diligent research he has uncovered some amazing new facts. Thanks to Brad, I am pleased to learn that I can continue to tell this story without having to fret about some educated feller correcting me.

It was a warm, sultry evening in Prescott on July 14, 1900. The saloons and gambling casinos along Whiskey Row were gearing up for a big Saturday night shindig. Gamblers were dealing cards, and the bargirls were hustling drinks. The rinky-tink sounds of piano music emanated from each raucous saloon. Boisterous, devil-may-care cowboys, railroaders and miners were bellying up to the bar for a night of revelry.

Yavapai County's famous citizen and lawman George Ruffner was heard to comment, "To jail all the drunks tonight, you'd have to put a roof over the whole town."

There was no time to lock up any drunks on this night, for a fire broke out and spread rapidly through the business district. Volunteer firemen pulling hose carts rushed out to fight the flames and save Whiskey Row. Folks grabbed what they could and rescued it from the raging fire. A barber hoisted his chair and his tools from the burning destruction and moved his business to the plaza's bandstand.

Up at the famous Palace Bar, loyal customers gallantly picked up the bar, and all its precious contents, and carried it across Montezuma Street, where the Yavapai County Courthouse sits today. Others picked up the piano and carried it to the safe environs of the plaza.

Prescottonians were not going to let something like a fire spoil their evening. So, while Prescott burned through the night, business resumed outdoors; resourceful bartenders served drinks, and the piano player banged away on the ivory keys. One of the painted ladies volunteered to sing.

And those frontier folks never lost their sense of humor either. By far, the most requested tune that evening was "There'll Be a Hot Time in the Old Town Tonight."

—Marshall Trimble
Arizona State Historian

ACKNOWLEDGEMENTS

Writing acknowledgements for this book proved very emotional for me. The process of researching and writing *The Whiskey Row Fire of 1900* has been one of the most challenging of my life. Not because of the research and writing—the project itself has been a blessing and distraction from life's inevitable trials. Researching and writing this treatise has been a joy.

In the middle of writing this newest installment of Whiskey Row history, I lost the great love of my life, Holly Joy Courtney, to a rare form of cancer. I was married to her for twenty-six wonderful years, but I have loved her since 1976. She was always the one. Forty-three years ago, something deep in my intuition told me, "There she is. That is her. The one! Go and get her." And I did. Of course, I understand now it was more than intuition, but something bigger than what is merely in front of us.

On January 31, 2018, I woke up from a nap to discover that her beautiful brown, doe-like eyes had turned a stunning gray. She had been promoted to Heaven. Her dying experience was glorious, although I begged God not to take her. She had lived her life seeking God, and for that she was rewarded with a wondrous dying grace.

This book is dedicated to Holly, an angel who flew too close to the ground. I was just one who recognized the truth of that description.

Auntie Caroline, I love you. We share a love for Holly, and we'll always have that beautiful link, old but youthful gal that you are, who I hope lives to one hundred–plus years.

Tom McCabe, no one could be a better friend than you are to me. Thank you for being there during my darkest moments these past two years.

Thank you, Joseph Sugrue, my pastor and friend, for your endless and priceless spiritual guidance.

Much gratitude for Lindsey Givens of The History Press for all of your encouragement and patience.

I want to thank Brenda "OK Girl" Taylor and Tom Schmidt of the Sharlot Hall Museum Library and Archives. A special thank-you goes to D. Sue Kissel, a phenomenal researcher.

Much gratitude is owed to Sue Tone of the *Daily Courier* for such invaluable editing. What would I do without you?

Danny Romero, the Whiskey Row balladeer, you are an inspiration. We have got songs to write.

Prescott historian Drew Desmond, your discoveries were very helpful. I look forward to working with you in future writings and presentations.

To Constable Ron Williams, thank you for being my partner in crime, for being my fellow Virgil Earp aficionado and helping me live history. We have got stuff to do.

Thank you, Wendi "Bradley" Roudybush for joining the Great Adventure with me. Your love and support have made the difference. You are the love of my "new life," and the cause of this glow my friends tell me that I have now. Those three words.

Dennis and Derry McCormick, owners of the Palace Restaurant and Saloon, your support and friendship honor me. Along with Scott Standford and Martha Mekeel, thank you for bringing the Palace Restaurant and Saloon to new heights and allowing me to "office" there with a glass of Hess Chardonnay from time to time.

Thank you, Dave Michelson, for making the Palace the go-to place on Whiskey Row for twenty-plus years. Because of you, it became more than a saloon and restaurant, but a museum-like, historical wonder.

As always, thank you to my son, Joshua Courtney, and my daughter, Lindsay "Bird" Courtney. What a fantastic blessing it is to be both your father and friend. I love the two of you so very much. Perhaps words exist to express that love. I am still looking for them.

INTRODUCTION

The burning of an entire city—a complete holocaust—is one of the most terrible things that the human mind is called upon to endure. Fire is our slave, and with jealous care, we keep it ever in bondage. But when it bursts its bonds and obtains the mastery, the devastation that issues is only to be compared with the breaking out of human slaves who have long been kept under cruel restraint; than which, in all ages, man has been able to conceive no greater horror.
—*The* Prospect, *January 1902*

Like the modern-day "big one," when the San Andreas Fault finally makes that dreaded big slip and wreaks its long-predicted devastation, a fire of frightening magnitude was not a question of "if" but "when" in young nineteenth-century Prescott.

In April 1888, a *Prescott Courier* (hereafter referred to as the *Courier*) editorial described the unrelenting danger: "The people of Prescott can look back and thank the gods that fire has not 'devoured' a great deal of their property. We now tell our people that the hot, dry season which may last until next July is upon us; that there will be windy days and nights when, should a fire get a good start, it would be hard to check." So it was that hot, dry night of July 14, 1900.

Modern-day Prescott and its famous Whiskey Row were shaped by three major fires. If the Whiskey Row fire of 2012 is counted, that makes four.

The fires of July 6, 1883, and February 14, 1884—both described in this volume—fashioned the Whiskey Row that was present on July 14, 1900.

During the evening of the latter date and the early morning thereafter, a fire ignited from a fallen candle that grew to nearly mythical dimensions and intensity. By the early morning of July 15, all that had been rebuilt after previous fires, and much more, was gone.

Prescottonians who witnessed Prescott's July 14–15 conflagration of 1900 often simply called it the "big fire." Sometimes it is referred to as the "Whiskey Row Fire," as reflected in the title of this book. That is because Whiskey Row—morphing into one version and then another throughout its early history and even after being rebuilt in 1901—was historically more than the quarter city block sectioned off today for visitors on Montezuma Street between Gurley and Goodwin Streets. It was a broader area, and the majority of it burned down that fateful evening.

It is true that Montezuma Street has always been the center of Whiskey Row—it is where the name originated. However, what was considered Whiskey Row over the decades often spilled over onto Cortez Street as it proceeded north from the plaza and east and west along Gurley and Goodwin Streets. Saloons lined the streets, extending the area characterized as Whiskey Row to include all of Prescott's infamous Block 13 (also called the 100 block), which included block-long portions of Goodwin, Gurley and Montezuma Streets and, of course, the red-light district on the east side of Granite Street parallel to Montezuma Street.

The main subject of this book, however, has most regularly been called the Great Fire of 1900 and so it shall be referred to throughout this book.

Great and terrible it was indeed. The *Arizona Weekly Journal-Miner* (hereafter referred to as the *Miner*), whose headquarters was one of the Great Fire's victims, claimed, "No such stroke as this had ever been laid on an Arizona town. In comparison, considering wealth and population, the much more famous Chicago fire of 1871 was an insignificant blaze, for little of Prescott remains but its homes." Almost all of Prescott's business district vanished in the flames. The heart of the mountain town was gone.

It has been called "an ill-fated night" and the greatest disaster in Prescott's history. Up to that point and long after, it surely was. Over and over, however, it has been said that the people of Prescott took the results in a philosophical, almost jubilant manner.

July 14, 1900, would prove to be the eve of rebirth for Prescott and its Whiskey Row, both refusing to be buried in their ashes. In fact, Prescott dates its current history from the Great Fire's ugly baptism.

With the birth of this Central Arizona Highlands hamlet in 1864, the seeds were planted for what became Whiskey Row. The rebirth of Prescott and Whiskey Row began immediately on July 15, 1900. Within a year's time, most of Prescott had been rebuilt in a much more substantial and aesthetic manner. The Great Fire was, without question, the pivotal event of Prescott history.

Today, residents and visitors are the benefactors, often unknowingly, of the resolve that fueled early twentieth-century Prescott's amazing rebuild—a Phoenix-like resurrection from flame and ash.

This volume details the beginnings of Arizona and Prescott, as well as the origins of Whiskey Row. This is followed by a description of the conditions and events leading up to Prescott's big inferno, then a six-chapter account of the Great Fire itself. Finally, there is a summary of the rebuilding of Prescott and Whiskey Row.

The author has chosen not to annotate but wants to assure the reader that he has painstakingly researched this subject with the absolute intent of discovering the truth, or at the very least, to arrive at historical probabilities. Instead, he has chosen to use the space such annotations would have occupied to tell the story of the Whiskey Row Fire of 1900 as completely as possible.

1

A TERRITORY AND PRESCOTT ARE BORN

For Whiskey Row to exist, there first had to be a Prescott, Arizona. Prescott would become one of the Old West's most significant frontier towns, but in early 1864, it was not even a notion. Hence, for there to be a Prescott, there first had to be an Arizona.

The United States Congress began bandying about the idea of Arizona as a separate territory in 1856. On February 24, 1863, while the United States was still fighting the Civil War, and after eighteen different congressional bill proposals, President Abraham Lincoln signed the Arizona Organic Act into law, establishing Arizona as a United States territory. It was finally dismembered from New Mexico Territory, which had been established in 1850.

However, this was not the first time there was a recognized Arizona Territory. It is necessary to look back further to get the full story. Before 1848, the land constituting what is now Arizona was part of the Republic of Mexico. Then came the Mexican-American War of 1846–48, resulting in United States victory. The Treaty of Guadalupe Hidalgo was signed on February 2, 1848. This gave the United States possession of most of present-day New Mexico and all but the most southern regions of what would eventually become Arizona, the United States' forty-eighth state. In 1850, legislators officially established this area as New Mexico Territory. Santa Fe was made its capital.

A border issue soon surfaced between the United States and Mexico. The Gila River initially formed the boundary between the two republics.

Both claimed ownership of the land just below it—an area that included a settlement called Tucson. President Franklin Pierce sought to end this dispute by sending a U.S. ambassador, James Gadsden, to Mexico City. He was instructed to purchase enough land from Mexico so that a transcontinental railroad could run through that section below the Gila. Gadsden's mission was successful. He negotiated a $10 million purchase of land consisting of 29,670 square miles that now make up southern Arizona and southwest New Mexico. That deal is known as the Gadsden Purchase.

Settlers who had moved into that region prior to the deal because of farming, ranching and mining opportunities, as well as those Mexicans who chose to stay behind and become American citizens, began clamoring for their own government and to make the Gadsden Purchase area a territory separate from New Mexico Territory. Santa Fe was too far away to be of any effective help to them. Furthermore, as one settler put it, there were "no laws for our guidance [and] no officers to preserve the peace."

Hoping to compel the U.S. government to hurry the process toward territorial status, the Gadsden Purchase inhabitants formed a provisional government in 1856 with Dr. Lewis Owings as governor and a full slate of territorial officers. The capital was to be either Tucson or Mesilla (today a town in New Mexico). They proposed that their section be called Arizona Territory. This was the first significant use of the name Arizona and the first effort to establish it as a separate entity.

The proposal was rejected.

While the U.S. Civil War was being fought, those still pushing for a separate territory saw an opportunity. Most of those residing in the Arizona portion of the New Mexico Territory—especially in its southern region—leaned toward Confederate thought. Hence, when Confederate colonel John Baylor rode in with a group of rough-and-tumble Texans and defined a Confederate Territory of Arizona and declared himself its military governor, most residents were pleased. On February 14, 1862, the Rebel government in Richmond, Virginia, accepted Baylor's definition and formally established the Confederate Territory of Arizona.

Baylor's tenure as governor, however, was short-lived. The president of the Confederate States of America, Jefferson Davis, ousted Baylor in early 1862 for blatantly ordering the genocide of the Apaches, who dominated the region. "Use all means to persuade the Apaches or any tribe to come in for the purpose of making peace, and when you get them together kill all the grown Indians and take the children prisoners and sell them to defray the expense of killing the adult Indians," Baylor had shockingly ordered.

The Confederate Territory of Arizona was also brief as an entity—eighty days to be exact. Circumstances changed after Union general James Carleton, with his First California Volunteer Infantry Regiment—commonly called the California Column—advanced into Arizona Territory in 1862. The Rebels were eventually pushed back to Texas. Tucson was captured by Union troops on May 20. For many, Tucson thus became the favored target for a future territorial capital location.

Like Baylor, General Carleton proclaimed himself military governor. Carleton's influence would play a major role in the formation of early Arizona. His negative opinion of Tucson would help turn a page in Arizona's Anglo-American history. Furthermore, there was an unmapped section of the newly declared territory that intrigued not only Carleton but also eventually those who President Lincoln sent Arizona Territory's way to establish a government.

After the Senate made Arizona Territory a new political entity on February 23, 1863, President Abraham Lincoln appointed a slate of ten territorial officers, an unusual, well-educated group of men assigned to set up a civil government. This contingent included John Gurley of Ohio, Lincoln's appointee for territorial governor. Gurley, however, died suddenly of appendicitis before he could make his way west. Lincoln replaced him with a New Englander, John Goodwin.

All but two of the chosen ten—commonly called the Governor's Party—joined Goodwin in Leavenworth, Kansas, on September 25, 1863. There, they launched a journey that would, unbeknownst to them at the time, eventually lead them to uncharted land in central Arizona Territory. Charles Poston, superintendent of Indian affairs for the new territory, and Milton Duffield, Arizona's United States marshal, did not travel with the main party. These two men left from San Francisco. Their destination? Tucson.

Although not stated in the congressionally accepted proposal for Arizona's territorial status, Tucson had repeatedly been proposed as the new province's capital while the issue was being deliberated over the years; it was assumed by many that would be Tucson's destiny. In the final bill, however, legislators removed Tucson as the capital site but not the unwritten assumption. The Governor's Party set its sights on Tucson.

The group headed toward the Santa Fe Trail. But three months before the group began the trek, events transpired in the new Arizona Territory that would eventually shift the thinking of those who would decide its fate and geographical make-up and would initiate events that still reverberate.

Before 1863, the Central Arizona Highlands were not designated on any extant map; it was a blank space. That changed when mountain man, scout and explorer Joseph Walker led an expedition of twenty-four men into the area. That spring, Walker's exploratory party found placer gold on the Hassayampa River, about six miles southwest of present-day Prescott. Other dream-seekers found gold a few miles east in Lynx Creek. Soon the general area was being called "the gold fields."

Although the Governor's Party was still three months from beginning its westward trek, General Carleton learned of the Walker party's gold discoveries and the other diggings. He soon became convinced that the Central Arizona Highlands was the region of Arizona's future, not "insignificant Tucson." He wrote to his military superiors, "It will be absolutely necessary to post troops in that section of the country." Then, with superb foresight, he penned, "Indeed the capital of Arizona will be sure to be established there."

After a surveying party filed a favorable report of the vicinity, Carleton sent troops ahead to establish a military presence to protect miners and the party of territorial officials now on their way. In the meantime, Carleton grew anxious to meet the appointed Arizona officials and feared that they "would never come."

The Governor's Party finally arrived at Fort Union, New Mexico Territory, on November 9, 1863. News of the gold findings in central Arizona had reached the party the week before, and Carleton met them ready to share more specific news and provide suggestions for a territorial capital site.

After hearing Carleton's report, gold fever struck the party. Governor Goodwin and his colleagues headed toward the Central Arizona Highlands and its prospective riches the next day. The site for the territorial capital, however, would not be known for another year. There was still much to consider.

While the Governor's Party made its way across New Mexico Territory, the army portion of the expedition went ahead toward the Central Arizona Highlands to set up a military presence. On December 23, 1863, Fort Whipple was established at Del Rio Springs in Little Chino Valley, where there was ample water and grass for livestock. The fort was named after a Union general, Amiel Weeks Whipple, who had surveyed across northern and southern Arizona in the 1850s but died of wounds suffered during the spring of 1863.

On December 29, four members of the Governor's Party finally reached Arizona Territory, arriving at Navajo Springs near today's Holbrook,

Richard McCormick was Arizona's first secretary of the territory and the founder of the *Arizona Miner*. *From Sharlot Hall Museum.*

Arizona. A hastily written proclamation stated: "The seat of government will for the present be at or near Fort Whipple." It was not until January 17, 1864, that the officials reached Whipple. Still more favorable reports of the mines were received during this time and read to the delight of all. Five days later, the rest of the party arrived, and soon a temporary capital was established at Del Rio Springs.

In February, Governor Goodwin began a journey across the territory to get to know it better and to officially pick a capital site. In April, he arrived in Tucson. In the meantime, at the behest of territorial secretary Richard

McCormick, gold seeker/scout Robert Groom and a small crew began platting a townsite with streets and blocks and lots within a relatively flat spot near Granite Creek, south of Little Chino Valley. Without official authorization, they had in their minds that this future settlement would be the site for a capital of the new territory.

By the time the governor returned to the highlands, further actions had been set in motion to establish a town around Granite Creek. Fort Whipple had been transplanted nearby to protect this sudden settlement, and a newspaper, the *Arizona Miner*, had been launched by McCormick at Whipple. A public meeting was announced for May 30 to look at Groom's townsite plans, and if accepted, "adopting the best mode of disposing lots in the proposed town."

The townsite as laid out by Groom was accepted during this meeting, and a name was given to the soon-to-be town. It would be named after the deceased historian William Hickling Prescott, who was revered by several members of Governor's Party. Street names like Montezuma, Cortez, Alarcon and Marina commemorated historical figures in his famous book *The Conquest of Mexico*. Gurley, Goodwin, McCormick and Carleton were also each honored with a street.

Another resolution with impact up to this very day was that "at least one square in the proposed town site should be reserved for a public plaza." Today it is called the Courthouse Plaza because it is graced by the magnificent Yavapai County Courthouse building. In 2008, it was named one of the greatest public places in America by the American Planning Association. It is the center of much activity, drawing people from all over Arizona, America and even the world. The plaza has a history of its own worth telling.

The biggest draw in Prescott over the decades, however, has been its famous Whiskey Row. Early Prescottonians did not necessarily want an area of their town named after whiskey, and for good reason. Those holding higher aspirations for their growing town were initially strongly opposed to this potent beverage that had infiltrated Prescott. It was altering the town in a way the townspeople deemed destructive and saw as a deterrent to outside visitation from capitalists and families and good Christian folk.

In the late 1860s and early 1870s, Prescott was in trouble. Prescott had lost the capital designation to Tucson. The three-year-old hamlet went into a tailspin. Report after report warned that something had to be done lest Prescott become lawless and unlivable for good people. An 1870 report cautioned that "indulgence in gambling, drinking, and other vices has been nearly as hard upon our people and country. But we have gone off our trail, and must now return." Lawlessness prevailed. Another report that

Robert Groom, Prescott's original surveyor, laid out plans for the soon-to-be mountain town and territorial capital. *From Sharlot Hall Museum.*

Today, the Courthouse Plaza is one of the great public places in the United States. *From Norman Fisk.*

same year stated that many believed saloons were a bad idea altogether. "We know our people would be better off were there no saloons in the Territory," editorialized the *Miner*.

Then there was the issue of a glaring absence of religion in Prescott. The soul of Prescott, many people thought, was facing a crisis point. In late 1870, the people at the *Miner* were increasingly worried and stated, "While the nice, attractive town is crowded with saloons it strikes the visitor's eyes that there is no church and not much Christian life and association." Visiting preachers tried to come to the rescue, but whiskey was winning the battle.

Saloons continued to multiply and with them came violence. Sylvester Mowry, an Arizona pioneer who sojourned in Prescott in 1871, documented, "Saloons 'till you can't rest' where they kill a man at least once a week. There was only one man killed at Prescott during my sojourn." *Only* one man. Mowry evidently viewed this as progress for Prescott.

During the 1870s—most likely beginning around 1874—residents of the downtown section along Montezuma Street began calling it "Whiskey Row." It was indeed a concentrated area where an inordinate amount of liquor was imbibed day after day and night after night.

This, as mentioned, was something many Prescottonians were not proud of at the time. Hence, Whiskey Row was absent from Prescott's papers for nineteen years. It was not until 1883 that the moniker found its way into print in a Prescott newspaper. And that was only after the district burned down, and it suddenly seemed appropriate to do so. The story of the Whiskey Row fire of 1883 is told in chapter 3 of this volume.

Outside newspapers, however, had no problem publishing the then-infamous name. The *Phenix Republican* printed the moniker twice before a Prescott newspaper felt it proper to do so—first on June 4, 1879, after a minor fire somewhere along the Row, and again on September 17, 1880, when it described how inebriants were dealt with along Prescott's drinking section. Somewhere along the Row a bucket of cold water was hidden above an entrance. Anyone going overboard with whiskey was led to it and doused with a painful pail full.

Although the name for which it would be known throughout the West probably originated in the 1870s, Whiskey Row's actual roots trace back to the year of Prescott's inception, 1864. When the government and practical business buildings went up that year and the next, so did Prescott's watering holes.

2

THE ORIGIN AND EVOLUTION
OF EARLY WHISKEY ROW

I t has been said that the history of the West was written in saloons, and to a
certain extent this declaration is not a lie. After all, saloons were the social
hubs of the Old West. In early Prescott, Arizona, this premise certainly
rang true. Less than a decade after 1864, Prescott would be identified as *the*
saloon town of Arizona Territory, in part because it was also predominately
a mining town.

It was in the saloon that gold and silver miners dropped their pickings on
weekends and sometimes weekdays, then journeyed out again to unearth
enough to spend during their next visit. It was the saloon owner who benefitted
most from the efforts of local miners. More often than not, a mine owner
would recognize this and become the proprietor of one or more saloons;
an inordinately high percentage of early Whiskey Row saloon owners had
connections to mining, sometimes owning several mines themselves. The
saloon was a type of gold mine unto itself.

Isaac Goldberg, a gold seeker from Poland who had drifted to the Central
Arizona Highlands after a short stay in La Paz, Arizona, saw an opportunity
to establish a saloon of sorts near Prescott, the newly formed capital of
Arizona Territory. Primitive like the new town it would serve, Goldberg's
saloon was Prescott's first. Goldberg had no name for his cantina, and for
decades it has been incorrectly identified by historians as the Quartz Rock
Saloon. As will be seen, there was a Quartz Rock Saloon that opened in
1864, but Goldberg had nothing to do with it.

Somewhere not too far from the main activities of town—probably on the banks of Granite Creek near the corner of Carleton and Goodwin Streets—Goldberg brought a collection of whiskies and set up his bar on a wooden plank straddling two barrels. On top of the bar he placed two bottles of whiskey and a tin cup.

For fifty cents, Goldberg sold his whiskey by the dram. That is not as cheap as it sounds. Today, fifty cents would have the purchasing power of between seven and eight dollars. Furthermore, a dram is but a splash, an eighth of an ounce—twelve drams can fit into one shot. A bottle of whiskey was a pure gold nugget.

A legend declares that Goldberg experienced some difficulty because some of his soused patrons stumbled and fell facedown into the creek trying to cross a makeshift bridge. The legend goes on to say that the proprietor moved his business northeastward to Montezuma Street. The relocated watering hole is said to have been the seed that germinated a row of saloons on Montezuma.

Whether drunken customers fell into Granite Creek cannot be known, but we now do know that Goldberg did not move his little bar to Montezuma Street. Instead, he moved his business to the Juniper House (described later) on the southeast corner of Cortez and Goodwin Streets. More saloons cropped up as it became clear Prescott was going to be the prominent Arizona Territory town of that time, especially because a civil government was being set up in Prescott in the summer of 1864.

Also, Prescott's first Fourth of July was approaching. Even though isolation caused shortages of both luxuries and necessities, Prescott's strongly pro-Union government and army officials believed it important to celebrate the birth of the United States. There was always the hope Arizona would, sooner rather than later, become a state. This expedited the "need" for suitable libation dispensaries.

When July 4 arrived, an estimated five hundred people were in town for the festivities. According to some narratives, they were all men. Miners from Lynx Creek and the Hassayampa River were among the celebrants. Secretary of the territory Richard McCormick's oration was the highlight of the planned program, and the Fort Whipple boys put on a nice show.

It was whiskey, though, that stole the day. Two "saloons" were identified as being present—those belonging to John Roundtree and John Dickson. Like Goldberg's setup, calling either of them actual saloons is a reach. Roundtree's outfit was nothing more than a wagon canvas stretched over two ponderosa pine poles covering a ten-gallon keg containing what one pioneer described as something akin to whiskey. You could not be sure what you were drinking in those days, but whatever it was usually contained an effective percentage of alcohol. Dickson's setup was a bit more refined, as it had the territory's first billiard table. It was probably housed in a quickly erected log structure facing the plaza on the northeast corner of Cortez and Goodwin Streets.

Both makeshift bars provided what patrons desired: a good time or outright intoxication. The eighth edition of the *Miner*, printed on July 6, 1864, reported, "We will not say how much whiskey was disposed of—it might surprise our temperate friends in Tucson and La Paz. Nobody was hurt, although the boys waxed very merry, and some of them very tipsy, and there was no little promiscuous firing of revolvers."

Receiving special attention in the *Miner*'s account of that day was George Barnard's Juniper House. Intriguingly, it was documented as Prescott's first restaurant and hotel, although no descriptions of said hotel exist. Where hotel residents slept is a mystery.

A map drawn several years later by a pioneer who was in Prescott in 1864—probably George Barnard himself—reveals what the Juniper House looked like. It was nothing more than a quickly erected, crude log structure. Pioneer Albert Banta called the Juniper House "a spacious dining hall." He followed that description by giving the room's dimensions: twelve by fifteen feet—no bigger than a small, modern-day bedroom.

Drawing of George Barnard's Juniper House, Prescott's first restaurant. *From Sharlot Hall Museum.*

Banta also described the dining table as being composed of ponderosa pine logs sawn in half lengthwise with the flat sides pushed together and facing upward. Problems arose when temperatures climbed, and the logs oozed sap.

It is possible that Isaac Goldberg sold whiskey out of the Juniper House during Prescott's first Independence Day. Barnard and Goldberg had both spent time in La Paz and probably knew each other while there. However, it was not until September 21 that Goldberg—the first liquor dealer to do so—placed an advertisement in the *Miner*, announcing that he was selling his liquors from the Juniper House. Furthermore, he informed Prescott that his libations were "warranted pure." Purity in whiskey or any other hard liquor was often suspect in the Old West. Prescottonians were glad to hear that something of better quality was now available.

That same issue of the *Miner* announced that one of Arizona's most noteworthy pioneers, William Hardy, after learning of the new capital in the Central Arizona Highlands, "lately made a hurried visit to Prescott with a view of opening a business establishment here." Hardy, founder of Hardyville (today's Bullhead City), did not want to miss out on the significant doings that came with a capital town. He had two businesses in mind to establish on the Granite Street portion of the 100 block, one of which is foundational to Whiskey Row history.

By October, residents learned that one of William Hardy's businesses would be a saloon. Hardy opened his unnamed bar on November 14 with great ceremony. The event was considered Prescott's first soiree. In attendance were John Goodwin, Richard McCormick, several members of the new Arizona House of Representatives and high-ranking officers from Fort Whipple.

There was reason to celebrate. The territory's first legislative session had concluded four days prior. Furthermore, to the delight of the gents in attendance, females were present. Around a dozen dancing partners made their way to Prescott and Hardy's new place.

On December 14, the people learned the name of Hardy's saloon: the Quartz Rock Saloon. Up until then, it was typically called "Hardy's new billiard saloon." Because of the establishment's fine billiard table, some said it was the best along the frontier. It also offered "a better class of liquors than we have been used to in Prescott." The Quartz Rock was the first saloon on a block—known then and today as either the 100 block or Block 13—that would contain an exorbitant number of saloons, even by Old West standards. It burned down in 1871 and was not rebuilt.

The Quartz Rock Saloon was Prescott's first go-to saloon. *From Bradley G. Courtney.*

The Quartz Rock "attracted much attention" and quickly became Prescott's go-to saloon. It remained so until 1868, when just one street east the next step in Whiskey Row's evolution arose on the southwest corner of Montezuma and Gurley Streets.

In the summer of 1868, Albert Noyes, owner of Prescott's first sawmill, began erecting a two-story edifice where Hotel St. Michael stands today on the corner of Montezuma and Gurley Streets. The upstairs was to be a meeting place for civic organizations and the bottom floor a saloon.

Left: Albert Noyes operated Prescott's first sawmill and built the "mammoth" building on the northwest corner of Montezuma and Gurley Streets that became the Diana Saloon. *From Sharlot Hall Museum.*

Right: Andrew Moeller, a former bartender and owner of the Quartz Rock Saloon, bought Albert Noyes's big building in 1868 and opened the Diana Saloon. *From Sharlot Hall Museum.*

After surviving two setbacks caused by monsoon weather, Noyes's nearly thirty-four-hundred-square-foot building was completed in October and stood taller than all other buildings in Prescott. Locals called it "an ornament to the town," and they expected "some Jolly old times inside its glittering walls."

Noyes, however, would never become a saloon man. He sold his big building for $8,500 (equal to more than $140,000 present day) to Andrew Moeller, nicknamed Doc, who had also bought the Quartz Rock from William Hardy in 1867. It was not until December 5 that Moeller held the grand opening of his saloon, which was still nameless at the time.

Opening night was a glorious affair. Most of Prescott was there. It was believed that Moeller's "new billiard and drinking saloon [was the] best finished and furnished saloon in the Territory," according to the *Miner*. It was not until the fall of 1869 that Moeller revealed the name of his establishment: Diana Saloon.

The Diana Saloon hosted at least three murders and a plethora of other violent episodes but was overwhelmingly Prescott's most popular meeting place until 1874. A succession of enterprises began to form to the south of

Above: This is believed to be the oldest image of Prescott, probably taken in the winter of 1869. The two-story Diana Saloon is left center. *From Sharlot Hall Museum.*

Right: The popular Diana Saloon became the cornerstone of early Whiskey Row. *From Sharlot Hall Museum.*

the Diana. Two other saloons grabbed their share of business: Jackson and Tompkins' and the Montezuma Saloon.

With the Diana as its cornerstone—making it the true mother of Whiskey Row—the evolution of a row of saloons hit a new stride when, just a few doors down, go-getter Dan Conner Thorne and his partner, William Hutchinson, opened the Cabinet Saloon at 118 Montezuma Street in the early summer of 1874. Described in the next chapter, it would become the heartbeat of early Whiskey Row. The Cabinet's spirit looms large along Whiskey Row even today.

3

A ROW IS NAMED AFTER WHISKEY AND THE BIRTH OF THE PALACE SALOON

Its names have been many, including the Palace Saloon, Palace Café and Palace Hotel. Today it is known as the Palace Restaurant and Saloon. This majestic slice of history was voted by *True West* magazine as the best of the West in 2018. Today, locals only have to say, "I will meet you at the Palace" at such and such time. No other explanation is needed because that means you will soon be walking through the bat-winged doors of 120 Montezuma Street.

If you sit near the front, you will watch tourist after tourist bust through those swinging doors like some Wild West outlaw or savior they may have seen portrayed in old westerns. They'll break into laughter before and after taking a picture or video of that same act.

You might end up on the back patio facing Whiskey Row Alley to smoke a cigarette or cigar. In earlier days, Whiskey Row Alley, situated between Whiskey Row and Prescott's red-light district, served as a meeting place for soiled doves and their clientele.

If you have reservations at the Palace, it might mean you will be seated in the special back-northwest section called the Bill Owens Room. This is the northwest portion of lot 19, at 118 Montezuma Street, a historic lot and address for reasons unknown to most Palace regulars but that are discussed later.

If you don't end up in one of those spaces, you might enjoy some first-rate food in the dining area where bullet holes can be seen in the ceiling, or you could sit in a booth named for one of the Earps, Doc Holliday or Big Nose Kate.

Many tourists walk in and their jaws drop. They feel as if they are in a time capsule with the Palace's mixture of vintage pictures on the wall, splendid specimens of elk heads above and museum-like displays all around. That feeling often stems from the fact that today's Palace looks much like it did when it was built in 1901. Some people choose only to look around, take pictures by the famous bar or swinging doors and then move on down Whiskey Row without sitting down for a drink or a fine meal.

For nearly three decades, the year 1877 has mistakenly been given for the Palace's beginning. The roots of this imposing restaurant and saloon actually trace back to 1874, making it by far the most vintage bar in Arizona. That, however, requires a surfeit of explanation. Along the way, the reader will also learn how an area chock-full of Prescott saloons became known as Whiskey Row.

THE CABINET SALOON AND ITS CONNECTION TO THE PALACE RESTAURANT AND SALOON

Dating back to 1874, the oldest bar in Arizona began with the man who probably had more influence upon early Whiskey Row history than any other: the dynamic Dan Conner (D.C.) Thorne. Today he is primarily known to local historians and a few Whiskey Row regulars, but in his time, he was a household name in Prescott. D.C. Thorne must be considered the original founder of the Palace Saloon.

Thorne was young Whiskey Row's most colorful character. With a force-of-nature personality and a ravenous lust for life, he created action, and action followed him wherever he went. He was one of the people who made Whiskey Row legendary, even in its own day. He helped give it a distinctive air.

A New Yorker, Thorne was one of the roughly 300,000 people lured to the West after news reached the eastern states that gold was discovered in California. Like many forty-niners, his endeavors were disappointing. In 1867, he moved to Prescott and quickly invested in several nearby mines. The Central Arizona Highlands proved to be what California was not. Thorne was soon on his way to finding fortune and realizing his dreams.

The first time Thorne's name appeared in the *Miner* was on January 1, 1870, when the newspaper reported that he had tied for first place with the

Dan Thorne, on the right, was perhaps early Whiskey Row's most influential figure. In the middle is Bob Brow, Palace Saloon's most well-known proprietor. *From Sharlot Hall Museum.*

future, and now infamous, sheriff of Cochise County, Johnny Behan, in a pigeon-shooting contest held on Christmas on the plaza.

Shortly after this, Thorne journeyed east to play a more serious game. He had boasted that he was going to "commit matrimony." His friends sniggered because, after all, he had no one in mind with whom to pledge such an oath. That did not stop Thorne. Sure enough, he met a nineteen-year-old New Jersey girl, Mary Wilson, along the way. On February 28, 1870, they married. By June, they were building a $2,000 house on North Montezuma Street.

It was in the summer of 1874 that Thorne began to make his true mark on Whiskey Row. He started to see profits from his mining ventures in the early 1870s, which enabled him to explore other entrepreneurial endeavors. He, along with William Hutchinson, opened the Cabinet Saloon on lot 19, 118 Montezuma Street, where the northern portion of today's Palace Restaurant and Saloon operates.

In the Cabinet Saloon's earliest years, Thorne kept an interesting mascot. The *Miner* informed, "Mr. D.C. Thorne has come into possession of a nice little pet in the shape of a cub bear, of the Cinnamon specie[s]. Dan has got the trick now wherewith to keep order in his usually well-regulated establishment. Should one or more of the billigerents [*sic*] become hostile and try to 'take the town' [the] young bruin will be turned loose, and if not able to command the peace, will at least be able to 'clean out' the crowd."

It was these types of attractions that made Thorne's Cabinet the forefront and trendsetter of Whiskey Row. He held raffles, lotteries and auctions and even ran a cockfighting pit on the Cabinet roof for a time. Thorne was never satisfied with the status quo and was constantly reinventing his saloon. Between 1874 and 1883, it was closed for repairs and improvements at least five times.

In 1877, Governor John Frémont's daughter, Lily, wrote in her diary, "[Thorne] keeps the chief faro & gambling place in the village, but is nevertheless a good citizen." Although it is impossible to pinpoint the exact beginning, it was around this time that the term "Whiskey Row" came into use.

Truly, the Cabinet Saloon would serve as the heartbeat of Whiskey Row for almost a quarter of a century and hosted unparalleled eighteenth-century saloon stories. The famous story of a baby left on the bar took place in the Cabinet, as well as the attempted murder of a woman by her jealous husband, with dynamite as the weapon. These stories are detailed in the predecessor to this book, *Prescott's Original Whiskey Row.*

Rally! Rally!
——TO THE——
GRAND OPENING
——OF——
The Cock Pit!
Friday Evening, Dec. 23,
Over the Cabinet Restaurant, to commence with a
General Maine of Game Cocks,
To be followed by Match Fights,
☞ DOORS OPEN AT 7 O'CLOCK. ☜
dec21-3t

D.C. Thorne sometimes held cockfights above his Cabinet Saloon. *From Sharlot Hall Museum.*

The Cabinet's fascinating history also includes three Earps (James, Virgil and Wyatt—Morgan was likely never in Prescott), Doc Holliday and his lady, Big Nose Kate. Their connection to Prescott and Whiskey Row is dealt with in the following chapter.

Because of a merger—described in the last chapter of this book—the Cabinet Saloon became the Palace Saloon in 1901 after the Great Fire. But there is much more to that story. There were three other Palace Saloons in early Prescott, though only one is related to today's Palace Restaurant and Saloon.

PIECING TOGETHER THE PALACE SALOON'S ORIGIN PUZZLE

In 1877, the first of Prescott's three Palace Saloons cropped up on 112 Gurley Street. This Palace Saloon was owned by Gilman Shaw and a United States marshal, Wiley Standefer—a member of the posse who would, along with Virgil Earp, gun down the outlaw George Wilson and his accomplice. It was a short-lived enterprise, lasting about one year before becoming a boot store. It has been incorrectly connected to today's Palace Saloon for many years due to incomplete research.

Another Palace Saloon sprang up on South Montezuma Street in 1883, owned by a Mrs. McManus—perhaps Whiskey Row's first female saloon proprietor. It lasted about a year before fizzling. Again, it has no connection to today's Palace Restaurant and Saloon.

The third Palace Saloon was established by Nathan Ellis and Al Whitney (who were also the latest owners of the aforementioned Diana Saloon) on Goodwin Street facing the plaza. It opened on June 23, 1883. Its origins are directly connected to today's Palace.

This Palace Saloon's story indirectly begins with the fact that throughout the late 1870s and early '80s, residents of Prescott were constantly aware that a first-class hotel was lacking in their somewhat remote town. They believed this absence kept visitors, including capitalists who might want to invest in their still young frontier town, from staying for any significant amount of time in Prescott. To be a "leading town," at least one first-class hotel was thought to be essential.

Almost weekly, a plea was found in the local newspapers to build a hotel that could represent the growing prosperity of Prescott. One from the *Miner* in the mid-1870s stated, "We will venture the assertion that there cannot be found in the United States a town with the number of inhabitants that Prescott has from two to three thousand without a hotel, while many have two or three."

Now and then, a lodging house—a far cry from a hotel—appeared, and the owners would claim that it was that long-desired establishment. In 1877, the Williams House touted itself as "the only first class hotel in town." Others saw it differently—it was neither large nor classy enough. The entreaties continued in the *Miner*: "Night after night strangers in Prescott are turned away from our various lodging houses for lack of room."

Certainly, there were several lodging houses in town, such as the Bit Saloon and Lodging House (which later became the Union Saloon) on the corner of Granite and Goodwin Streets, a red-light district mainstay. Its advertisements underscored clean beds in rooms that were actually tiny "cribs" just big enough for a bed and walking space for two people. These rooms rented for anywhere between twenty-five and fifty cents. Even the most naïve Prescottonian knew of the kind of transactions prostitutes carried out in these rooms.

Then there were establishments like Dan Hatz's Pioneer Hotel and Bakery, located on the corner of Montezuma and Goodwin Streets. There, one could get a room for a week for eight dollars and three meals for fifty cents a day. These types of rooms, limited in number, were often already

The Union Saloon and Lodging House, on the southeast corner of Granite and Goodwin Streets, ran ads that underscored clean beds. *From Sharlot Hall Museum.*

taken by long-term boarders. Something bigger and better was called for. The dilemma was declared solved in April 1883, when Moses Hazeltine Sherman from New Hampshire opened the Sherman House on Goodwin Street facing the south end of the plaza.

The people of Prescott immediately saw the Sherman House as something special. The *Courier* and people of Prescott "expressed delight at beholding so good a hotel in this frontier town." Nathan Ellis and Al Whitney, the most recent owners of the still-flourishing Diana Saloon, saw an opportunity too good to pass up. They predicted that the Sherman House would attract a large clientele. A saloon near it would certainly benefit from this. They decided to build one as part of the Sherman Block.

Ellis was the spokesperson for this undertaking. The public watched with interest as Prescott's latest "resort" arose. As it neared completion, all noticed it was lacking two main ingredients, both of which residents had been crying out for since Prescott's inception.

The *Courier's* take on this would unfortunately prove prophetic: "N. Ellis says that he will make [his new saloon] both useful and ornamental and yet we sigh for a stone or brick structure." Ellis responded by pointing his finger at other Prescott business owners still using lumber for their structures. When they switch to brick and stone and mortar, he retorted, so would he and his co-proprietor, Whitney. Even the brand-new Sherman House was constructed of wood.

The original Palace Saloon was located two doors over from the two-story Sherman House. Its external appearance was rather lackluster, but the interior was ostentatious. *From Sharlot Hall Museum.*

On Saturday, June 23, 1883, Prescott's newest saloon opened in grand fashion. With a bottle of champagne, it was christened "The Palace." It was touted as not only the largest saloon in northern Arizona but also, in refinement, the finest in the Southwest.

Conspicuously, the Palace's exterior was not palatial, even by the standards of that time. In fact, it was ordinary. Once inside, though, locals felt they were inside a veritable palace. It radiated pretension. The walls were ornamented with gold-colored paper. Sundry oil paintings of various natural landscapes were featured in every room. There was a reading room and a club room, and three billiard tables were installed in a room toward the back.

The Palace was an instant success; it drew large crowds on a nightly basis. Two weeks after its grand opening, by a terrible twist of fate, the Palace Saloon would become even more in demand.

THE WHISKEY ROW FIRE OF 1883

In the town's first nineteen years, the 1883 fire was "the most destructive fire that has ever been Prescott's misfortune to experience." It was a Friday morning, July 6, 1883, when the courthouse bell sounded. Fire! When it was all over, most of what was then identified as Whiskey Row was gone.

To understand this fire, it is necessary to explain why Prescott was so vulnerable to terrible fires right up until 1900. Unfavorable conditions and

BIG BLAZE IN PRES-COTT.

Whisky Row Licked up by Flames.

Hundreds Houseless and Homeless.

Loss about $100,000.

After the Montezuma Street fire of 1883, the term "Whisky Row" first appeared in a Prescott newspaper. *From Bradley G. Courtney.*

factors in fledgling Prescott made fire prevention and firefighting a challenge. Like modern strip malls, the businesses along Whiskey Row were attached, which was not uncommon in the West. However, the major difference between the strip malls of today and the businesses of Prescott's early days is that they were generally strung together by wood. If one business caught fire, it was likely that those adjacent would ignite, setting off a domino effect.

Also, in the Prescott of 1883, many of the wooden edifices along Whiskey Row—including the structure housing the Cabinet Saloon—were some of the oldest in town, dating back to 1865–66. Up the street, the Diana Saloon still stood tall but with lumber that was probably untreated and at least fifteen years old.

Another issue was the type of lumber used to assemble the houses in early Prescott and Whiskey Row—ponderosa pine, the wood of the West, which dominates the forest encompassing Prescott. In fact, the forest in which Prescott is situated is part of the largest stand of ponderosa pines in the world. For expediency's sake, it became the building material of choice in young Prescott. But it had its problems.

Although ponderosa pine trees are highly resistant to fire in their natural state, once the bark is stripped from a ponderosa and the tree becomes lumber, it loses that advantage. For the most part, the bark is what is resistant to fire. Furthermore, ponderosa pine lumber, if untreated, is prone to decay, leading to an extremely low resistance to fire. Even if ponderosa pine lumber is treated, the methods of doing so in the 1860s and '70s, when the earliest Prescott and Whiskey Row buildings in question were first built, were largely ineffective. Wood preservation was a rather poorly developed science in those days. In Prescott's case, because of the need to quickly build not only a town but also a territorial capital, the odds lean heavily toward untreated lumber. Also, many of early Prescott's lumbermen were beginners in the profession, learning that trade as they went along. Wood preservation took a back seat during that learning process.

The final issue that made Prescott predisposed to disaster is that pre-1901 Prescott often had an inadequate water supply. Unlike most American climatic zones, where April showers bring May flowers, April and May in the highlands of central Arizona are the third- and second-sparsest months, respectively, for rainfall. June and early July often totally lack rainfall. The spring and very early summer of 1883 (and 1900, as will be seen later) were no different.

Soon after the alarms had sounded in downtown Prescott around 8:30 a.m. on July 6, 1883, the boom of cannon from Fort Whipple north of town was heard. The army's hook and ladder truck rushed toward the smoke. Citizens hurried from every direction toward the Cabinet Saloon—some to help fight the fire, and some just to gawk.

Smoke poured from the windows and doors of the Cabinet's restaurant section, located to the rear of the saloon, where the fire originally ignited. "Fire, like the Apaches, comes when least expected," the *Courier* reported the next day. Flames quickly burst through the restaurant's rooftop and soon the Cabinet Saloon itself. A defective flue connected to the Cabinet kitchen was later cited as the source of the fire.

Volunteer firefighters hastily directed streams of water toward the flames, but the fire was already building in intensity. A nearly equal amount of smoke was now issuing from neighboring buildings. The monsoon season had arrived the night before, and the increased humidity had helped keep the roofs of the buildings damp. It had rained almost the entire night of July 5 and well into the early morning of July 6. Had this not been part of the equation, a different story might be told here.

Despite the seasonal rains, the fire's momentum continued. Almost every fire in Prescott's history has felt the effect of winds blowing from the south. On this morning, however, there was a preponderant calm, and winds were generally still. Yet the fire, with its burgeoning ferocity, was spreading both north and south. The chief worry was the fire's northward path, which seemed more resolute, just as it would on July 14, 1900. Up Montezuma Street the fire raged.

The Cabinet Saloon burned to the ground. The old Montezuma Saloon two doors north bowed to the flames, as did the Arcade Brewery, Fred Hubbard's cigar shop, J.L. Fisher's auction store and Bones and Spencer's fruit store. Next in line was Ellis and Whitney's popular Diana Saloon on the southwest corner of Montezuma and Gurley Streets.

Firefighters were forced to make a decision because not only Whiskey Row but also the town itself was now in danger. If the Diana ignited, there was a strong chance that the inferno would jump Gurley Street. The Kelly and

Stephen's store across the street was full of flammable items: clothing, furniture, tobacco products, stationery and newspapers. If it caught fire, the domino effect was likely to continue, with a chance of taking over the entire town.

All hands available and willing started emptying the Kelly and Stephen's store. Some soaked the carpets and blankets with water. Cotesworth Head, owner of the mercantile store on the northeast corner of Gurley and Montezuma, also began preventive measures. He ordered the dismantling of the wooden balcony wrapped around his store.

The fire had grown so intense, however, that it was thought these measures would only mitigate damages should the fire cross Gurley Street. Was there a way to limit the fire's path to Montezuma Street below Gurley Street? Was blowing up the Diana Saloon the best bet to stop the fire? A quick decision was needed. Since the Diana was surely fated to burn, the choice was not a difficult one to make.

John Kirwagen, a cattle rancher, volunteered to perform the critical work. He placed fifty pounds of "giant powder"—nitroglycerin and kieselguhr—at the lowest levels of the Diana. While Kirwagen was working and hurrying to beat the fire before it devoured the saloon, citizens ran into the Diana to remove "fixtures and chattels." When all was set, Kirwagen lit the fuse. The rancher's efforts bore perfect fruit. The Diana toppled neatly to the ground. Firefighters instantly sprayed its old lumber with water. The conflagration's northward trek was halted in its tracks.

The southward advance of the blaze found its deterrent already in place. John Greenway Campbell had run a successful mercantile store on mid-Montezuma Street since 1866. The forward-thinking Campbell acted with extraordinary foresight when he constructed one of Prescott's first stone-and-brick buildings—the first "fireproof" structure on Whiskey Row. In fact, any business neighboring Campbell's store was quick to advertise that it was right next to this theoretically fireproof structure.

Indeed, Campbell's edifice proved invaluable on this July morning and gave credence to the oft-made argument that it would be wise to build stone-and-brick structures in Prescott. When the fire hit Campbell's store just two lots before the Cabinet Saloon, a negligible amount of wood was present to feed those flames. Stone and brick proved worthy opponents. A bucket brigade formed in front of the store. Flame eventually fed on nothing but flame. The southward advance of the fire stopped.

The fire of 1883 was the first of three fires that would affect the geography of Whiskey Row—the Whiskey Row that was present on July 14, 1900, and even the Whiskey Row of today.

D.C. Thorne's already legendary Cabinet Saloon was gone. So was Nathan Ellis and Al Whitney's Diana Saloon, the saloon that begat all other Montezuma Street saloons. All was not lost for this pair, though. With most of the Montezuma Street saloons in ashes, their new Palace Saloon on Goodwin Street—only two weeks old at the time of Prescott's first major Whiskey Row fire—now had no legitimate competition.

Seven months after the 1883 fire, another major fire struck Goodwin Street's Sherman block. It, too, affected Whiskey Row's history in a way that echoes to this day. But before describing this fire, it is time to pause to take a look at the Earps, Doc Holliday and their Prescott/Whiskey Row/Tombstone connection. Much has been conjectured—and exploited—regarding them and Whiskey Row; therefore, the subject, at long last, needs to be addressed.

4

THE EARPS, DOC HOLLIDAY AND WHISKEY ROW—FOLKLORE VERSUS "FACTLORE"

Walking along Whiskey Row today, one's ears are bombarded from passersby chattering about Wyatt Earp and Doc Holliday, and for good measure, the other Earp brothers and Doc's lady, Big Nose Kate, because "they were here." It becomes even more intense when sitting in one of the Row's saloons, especially the Palace Restaurant and Saloon, where it is said the OK Corral legends sat. Is it true? Yes.

But clarification and amplification are needed. Truth is always good in the end, although it may be bothersome. In this case—because of the fascination with the Earps and Doc Holliday among western history buffs—it works well for Prescott, Whiskey Row and the Palace Restaurant and Saloon.

About the issue of these historical icons patronizing the Palace, one current patron put it this way: "If you put a GPS on it, it will prove close enough." That is certainly true and insightful, but as always, there is more to the story. One must once again understand the relationship between the pre-fire Cabinet Saloon and today's Palace Restaurant and Saloon. The two cannot be historically separated.

As mentioned, three Earps and Doc Holliday were customers—surely more than once—at the Cabinet Saloon at 118 Montezuma Street (where the north section of today's Palace is situated), Whiskey Row's most popular resort at that time. Virgil Earp was there as early as 1877, Wyatt and James in late 1879 and Doc Holliday in 1879 and most of 1880. It is likely that

Doc did very well playing poker in the Cabinet. Hence, the famous early-on movie scene in *Tombstone*.

Virgil may have visited a Palace Saloon in 1877—the one on Gurley Street previously described, which is not related to today's Palace. However, when Wyatt and Doc were in Prescott, no saloon called the Palace existed in Prescott. The Cabinet Saloon—forerunner to today's Palace Restaurant and Saloon—did. And it was the go-to place along Whiskey Row when the Earps and Doc were here.

Since the Cabinet's proprietors, Barney Smith and Ben Belcher, joined forces with Palace proprietor Bob Brow to form the post–Great Fire Palace Saloon, and the Cabinet Saloon became the Palace Saloon, it can be claimed that the Tombstone boys did indeed visit the Palace but obviously not in its present form.

The Earps—especially Wyatt—and Doc Holliday, have become peculiarly ubiquitous in western folklore. The author has been to more than one modern western saloon where it was claimed that Wyatt and Doc sat right here at their bar and drank, only to discover that neither of them had ever been near said town of said saloon.

There is a story that has been spread throughout Whiskey Row, and its origin is a total mystery. It has hit Wikipedia's unstoppable train and has even been published in a major newspaper. It is a tale of Wyatt easily gunning down two men on Whiskey Row Alley behind the Palace for reasons unknown. Not even a remote possibility.

As Marshal Trimble, Arizona's state historian, told this author, "There is a lot of 'folklore vs. factlore' when it comes to portraying history, especially western history." Truth is, when Wyatt visited Prescott in late 1879 and stayed for probably no more than a month, his name never appeared in any of the local newspapers. In fact, it is likely that few knew who he was. His presence in Prescott was not newsworthy at the time, although in the minds of many today, it was. It is a totally understandable phenomenon.

However, the first time Wyatt appeared in a Prescott newspaper was after the now celebrated OK Corral gunfight, and it was not complimentary to him or his brothers or Doc Holliday. Wyatt's older brother, Virgil, however, made news in Prescott in a spectacular manner on October 17, 1877.

VIRGIL EARP'S CAREER AS A LAWMAN BEGINS IN PRESCOTT

So great is the shadow cast by Tombstone's legendary 1881 shootout at the OK Corral that it is not widely known that Virgil Earp's law-enforcement career began in Prescott. Its launching point was a prominent saloon along Whiskey Row.

In 1877, the Jackson & Tompkins' Saloon, at 134 South Montezuma Street and near the center of Whiskey Row, was one of the top four saloons in Prescott. On October 17 of that year, Colonel William McCall, a Pennsylvanian who had been brevetted general during the Civil War, was enjoying a game of billiards. Two men, George Wilson (calling himself "Mr. Vaughn") and Robert Tullos (also known as John Tallos), walked in and made a beeline for McCall. One jabbed a pistol in his back while the other whispered threats in the colonel's ear, something like, "Keep your mouth shut or else!"

Why convey such a warning? A few months prior, McCall had been living near the Texas/Oklahoma border. While there, he learned Wilson had murdered Robert Broddus (sometimes spelled Broaddus), deputy sheriff of Montague County, Texas. Very possibly, McCall played a part in chasing Wilson, who proved elusive. The murderer fled to Colorado before journeying to Prescott. To Wilson's surprise, and knowing McCall was aware of his crime, he spotted McCall and was concerned the colonel might cause him trouble.

The killing occurred when Deputy Sheriff Broddus was escorting Wilson from Collin County to Montague County to stand trial for an undisclosed misdemeanor. With Broddus were two guards: Bud McGary and Tom Lemans. The three lawmen and the prisoner were camping one spring morning in Denton County along Bolivar Creek. The guards were making breakfast. Suddenly, Wilson grabbed McGary's gun, pulled the trigger and shot Broddus to death. He then snatched Broddus's horse.

Apparently, Wilson had at least a smidgen of scruples. Before escaping, still holding his gun on them, Wilson offered McGary and Lemans twenty dollars for a saddle. The guards refused but, bafflingly, sold a pistol to the outlaw for ten dollars, then gave him a blanket so that he would not have to ride bareback on Broddus's horse.

On June 2, 1877, Texas governor Richard Hubbard offered $500 for the capture or death of Wilson. He would up the ante in November, but by then, it was of no consequence.

Back in Jackson & Tompkins', Colonel McCall somehow escaped and dashed straight into the office of Justice of Peace C.F. Cate and reported the presence of the outlaws. Cate issued an arrest warrant for Mr. Vaughn and John Doe; Tullos was a stranger to McCall, and perhaps McCall really believed Wilson's last name was Vaughn. Cate gave the warrant to Constable Frank Murray, who immediately strode over to Jackson & Tompkins', followed by McCall.

Prior to their arrival, the two no-goods—clearly soused—had stepped outside, and one took a potshot at a woman's dog as they strolled along Prescott's plaza. When Murray arrived, the scoundrels believed they were being held accountable for discharging the gun at the animal. Told otherwise, both drew their pistols, quickly mounted up and galloped their horses south down Montezuma while shooting to the left and right, like a scene from a wild western movie.

Murray gathered an all-star posse, but it took a bit of time, which gave the desperadoes a good head start. Somewhere in Prescott, three men were engaged in friendly conversation, though they were far enough away to be oblivious to what just transpired. Two were high-ranking lawmen: Yavapai County sheriff Ed Bowers and U.S. marshal Wiley Standefer. It is likely that these lawmen would have hurried to the sound of gunfire had they been close enough to hear it.

When they were gathered, Bowers and Murray took up the chase on horseback. Standefer and McCall hopped aboard the marshal's horse-drawn carriage. The third man was Virgil Earp, who was new to Prescott and so little-known that the *Miner* repeatedly reported his name as "Mr. Earb." He was toting his Winchester rifle, and given the situation, it might come in handy.

Most Old West historians—including Earp's biographer, Don Chaput—believe that Virgil had not been an official lawman up to this point. Virgil claimed that he served in some capacity as a lawman in Dodge City, Kansas, with his brother Wyatt. There is no documentation verifying this.

Virgil must have made an impression upon the three lawmen; the Union army veteran was promptly deputized. But Earp had no horse at the time, and there was room for only two on the carriage. He would have to keep up on foot.

Wilson and Tullos were expected to be far down the trail by now. How long could Virgil last? Fortunately for him, the chase would not be a long, heroic, western movie–like affair but more like a scene from Mel Brooks's *Blazing Saddles*. The outlaws, instead of distancing themselves from Prescott, stopped about a half mile (perhaps less) southwest of the Row, probably on the corner of Carleton and Granite Streets by Prescott's main waterway Granite Creek. Both dismounted with pistols pulled. They lit cigarettes and waited.

Standefer and McCall, leading the posse and moving fast, rode right by the fugitives. This was a lucky break for the outlaws, until one of them shouted, "Don't run over us, you s— of a b—!"

Imagine what the other outlaw thought at this outburst.

The two posse members halted, jumped off the carriage and turned their pistols on the bad men. Murray and Bowers, riding down from the north, dismounted and did the same. Earp quickly caught up, positioned himself between the four other lawmen and shouldered his Winchester. Hearing the demand to surrender, Wilson vociferously entreated God, "O' Lord have mercy on me, a poor drunken, worthless d—d son of a b—."

The criminals opened fire. Bullets and buckshot came from three directions. Wilson fell immediately when a bullet penetrated his skull. Tullos died instantly after being shot eight times. Most, if not all, of those wounds came from Virgil's Winchester.

To the astonishment of many, George Wilson hung on for two days with a bullet lodged in his head. The *Miner* boys turned theological those two days, wondering if the prayer Wilson bellowed before being shot had any effect because of the sincerity behind it—even with its profanity. "It was the language with which he was familiar. The question is, are not such earnest prayers as likely to be answered as those hypocritically expressed in more elegant phrase?" the *Miner* speculated. All for naught. Wilson died with a bullet still in his brain.

An interesting side note to this story is that Virgil's younger brother, Wyatt, had dealt with Wilson in Wichita, Kansas, in 1875 when he was a policeman. Apparently, Wilson had "forgotten" to pay for a wagon he had acquired. Wyatt came to collect and did so after a bit of firm prompting. Small world. Small Old West world.

It was later learned that Wilson was eviler than first thought. He was also wanted for the murders of the sheriff and deputy sheriff of Las Animas County, Colorado.

This episode proved to Prescottonians that Virgil was a man who could be counted on and that he was a crack shot with a rifle. He was soon appointed Prescott's night watchman and was elected constable in 1878. Ironically, he defeated the very man, Frank Murray, who made him a member of the October 17 posse.

Late in 1879, after a series of correspondences between the brothers, Wyatt and older brother James arrived in Prescott with their wives. In late December 1879, Virgil and Wyatt arrived in Tombstone, the territory's latest boomtown. Morgan most likely arrived sometime in the spring of 1880. Doc Holliday, ever the sporting man, stayed in Prescott for at least eight months to gamble on Whiskey Row. On October 26, 1880, in a thirty-second gunfight, the four friends shot their way into eternal fame.

5

THE SHERMAN BLOCK FIRE AND THE FIRST RESURRECTION OF WHISKEY ROW

After the Whiskey Row fire of July 6, 1883, fewer saloons graced Prescott's Row. The Palace Saloon drew a majority of the displaced business. The Sazerac Saloon on Gurley Street also became more popular.

A new business, Cob Web Hall, appeared at 140 Montezuma Street and would become famous for a saloon story—often called Arizona's most famous saloon story—that was said to have taken place therein but in fact transpired in the Cabinet Saloon. This story is elaborated on in *Prescott's Original Whiskey Row*, the predecessor to this volume. Nevertheless, Cob Web Hall became known for attracting a more sophisticated, educated clientele than other Whiskey Row haunts.

Much of the burned-out portion of the 100 Block's Montezuma Street still had empty lots available in February 1884. There would be more empty lots, this time on Goodwin Street, after Valentine's Day. The sound of the fire alarm very early on that morning, February 14, 1884, created déjà vu for the people of Prescott. The origin of this fire was in the first-class hotel of which Prescottonians were so proud, the Sherman House. Like the Whiskey Row fire of 1883, a defective flue was the cause.

By the time firefighters arrived, flames were already overwhelming the less-than-one-year-old building. There was one casualty. The rest of its guests "barely escaped with their lives." One of the guests was the newest editor and owner of the *Miner*, Samuel Nelson Holmes, who was staying on the second floor of the Sherman House with his wife. When the fire was

"WHISKEY ROW" including "COB WEB HALL"

Cob Web Hall was a Whiskey Row saloon that was known for attracting a more sophisticated clientele. *From Sharlot Hall Museum.*

first spotted, Holmes was not in his room. It is not known where he was, though some people believed he had been outside of the Sherman House and somewhere on Goodwin Street. His wife was perhaps the first to notice the trouble and is credited with running from room to room, warning guests of the swelling fire and surely saving their lives.

The *Miner* poetically reported, "Along the wooden and papered walls the forked tongues of fire leaped and chased each other with demonized and resistless fury." Soon the Sherman House was hopelessly overwhelmed with flames. Its immediate and highly flammable neighboring businesses, J.W. Wilson's clothing store to the east and J.L. Fisher's auction house to the west, were helpless and quickly caught fire. People watching from the hills above Prescott declared that they had never seen a larger body of flames.

Also in grave danger was the business adjacent to Wilson's: Nathan Ellis and Al Whitney's popular Palace Saloon. The Palace was still open when the fire started. Inside were Whitney and bartender Julian Percy. With assistance, they pulled out the bar, one billiard table and a piano before the Palace was consumed by the blaze.

Now the entire street block, composed of sections of Goodwin, Cortez, Carleton and Montezuma Streets, was in danger of being devoured. Prescott's vaunted chief of police at that time, James Dodson, took charge.

Remembering how well the dynamiting of the Diana Saloon had worked during Whiskey Row's 1883 fire, Dodson began blowing up the surrounding buildings. These measures were successful; "the limits of the fire had been fixed and its further spreading made impossible," reported the *Miner*. But the entire Sherman Block burned to the ground.

After the conflagration was quelled, a dreadful fear took hold. Samuel Holmes was missing. Someone said they saw him running into the Sherman House when it was ablaze, probably with the aim of saving his wife. When the Sherman House ashes had cooled, the remains of a barely recognizable human being were found. Later, a shirtsleeve's studs and buttons identified their wearer as those belonging to the *Miner* owner.

Two separate areas now existed in Prescott with empty lots due to two conflagrations. This was perhaps the third most important span of time in Prescott's history—the first being its founding in 1864 and the second after the Great Fire of 1900. With much of the Montezuma Street's old Whiskey Row still vacant and now Goodwin Street's Sherman Block gone, Prescott had an opportunity to replace it with something better. Whiskey Row was ripe for a second life.

Another new saloon, the Eclipse, appeared on Montezuma Street in February 1884. It would not last long, but with its arrival came one of the Row's most famous proprietors, Robert Brow. His name is the one most associated with the early days of the Palace Saloon.

WHO WAS ROBERT BROW?

Robert "Bob" Brow, born circa 1857 in Missouri, was a true western pioneer. In the early 1870s, when Robert was in his mid-teens, and after a sojourn in Nebraska, Brow's father, Jacob, moved the family to the Dakota Territory. They stayed for a short time in its capital city, Yankton.

In 1875, the adventurous Brows journeyed into the Black Hills, a region now part of western South Dakota. John Pierson found gold in a narrow canyon of the northern Black Hills called Deadwood Gulch, and a gold rush ensued. This area was still considered Lakota Indian land, but that did not stop an illegal Anglo invasion.

Jacob saw an opportunity in Deadwood Gulch. He and his sons—Bob was now in his late teens—joined an expedition of miners in a supplementary role. Brow bought a sawmill of the crudest type to set up wherever the miners decided to work and settle. On the way there, however, the Lakota attacked the expedition. Jacob Brow fought so heroically against them that it brought him national recognition.

Although injured in the Lakota confrontation, Jacob recovered and began operating his sawmill in Deadwood Gulch—soon to be the site for the legendary town of Deadwood. He was first to do so and was soon putting out lumber for the boys seeking gold.

In 1881, the twenty-something Bob Brow grew tired of the lawlessness in Deadwood and was ready to venture into the world. He and a companion set out for another boomtown: Tombstone, Arizona. Coming down through Utah, he entered Arizona Territory and crossed the Colorado River via Lee's Ferry. Along the way, Brow changed his destination. He would not go to Tombstone after all, though this would have put him there at the same time as the

Bob Brow is probably the proprietor most often associated with the early days of the Palace Saloon. *From Sharlot Hall Museum.*

Earp brothers and Doc Holliday. Brow learned that the Atlantic and Pacific Railroad was being built and would run through Holbrook, slightly east and near the center of the territory.

On the way to Holbrook, famished and thirsty to the point that they thought they might perish, he and his chum dragged themselves into Holbrook to recover. The two soon won a contract with the railroad, doing work of an undisclosed nature. That work led Brow west toward the Colorado River on the California and Arizona Territory border. He engaged in a variety of businesses before heading toward the Central Arizona Highlands and Yavapai County area in 1883.

In 1886, Brow took part in another building project. This time it was thirty-three miles south and slightly west of Prescott, near a tiny community called Walnut Grove. A loose rock dam was being built to provide water for placer miners and to help farmers below the dam irrigate five hundred acres of land. Brow was heavily involved in the building of the dam. He stayed connected to the operation and maintenance, but it was doomed. In

1890, Walnut Grove Dam broke due to poor construction, which left Brow in near financial ruin.

This disaster eventually led Brow to Prescott, where he soon became a household name and a historic figure still known by many in Prescott and Arizona today.

THE NEW WHISKEY ROW TAKES SHAPE

After two major fires, Whiskey Row was at a crossroads in 1883 and 1884. Would it be rebuilt and become an area sponsoring more innocuous purposes? Or would it become a grander version of what it once was and had become famous for throughout the West?

Palace owners Nathan Ellis and Al Whitney must have felt cursed, having lost to fire two of the most popular saloons in Prescott, the Diana and Palace Saloons, within a span of seven months. The Palace's losses amounted to $8,000. They received $5,000 from insurance, giving them at least a fighting chance to rebuild. Although both owners were hesitant, Prescott's newest newspaper at the time, the *Courier*, virtually begged them to reestablish the Palace, hoping they would "shortly secure a good business location and start again, to grow up with the country."

About a month after the Sherman Block fire, Ellis and Whitney announced that they would rebuild but not on Goodwin Street. They moved their saloon to Montezuma Street. The location they chose was one the Palace would, in effect, never leave—in fact, it would expand from that spot after the Great Fire. They reopened as soon as possible at 118 Montezuma Street, lot 19, where D.C. Thorne's celebrated Cabinet Saloon had operated for nine years. Today, this is the northern section of the Palace Restaurant and Saloon.

The Palace reopened on July 4, 1884, when Prescott was already in the mood to celebrate. An estimated one thousand people came to see the new eighty-by-twenty-five-foot edifice. A band played near the entrance to mark the importance of the event. To the satisfaction of many, every measure was taken by Ellis and Whitney to make the new Palace as fireproof as possible—a stone foundation, brick walls, an iron roof and iron shutters.

The bar that was pulled out of the Goodwin Street Palace by Al Whitney and Julian Percy during the 1884 Sherman Block fire was reinstalled, but its days were numbered. Frank Parker was commissioned to build a bar of solid walnut. Installed immediately after its construction, it would remain in the Palace Saloon until 1897, when another bar took its place, survived the Great Fire and became a legend. That story is disclosed in greater detail in chapter 10.

On September 30, 1886, D.C. Thorne and Pete Kastner reopened the Cabinet Saloon on lot 21, 122 Montezuma Street, at great expense. The southern end of the Palace Restaurant and Saloon is located there today. Thorne switched his loyalties in 1888. He sold the Cabinet and became the proprietor of the Palace Saloon, two doors north. He kept it until 1891.

In 1892, Bob Brow began his legendary stint with the Palace when he purchased a 50 percent interest. He immediately expanded the saloon's restaurant, which eventually featured Prescott's most extensive menu, offering full meals for twenty-five or fifty cents. It became the place where men went to enjoy cigars and libations, gamble and socialize, do business, look for work, sell mining claims and, on occasion, vote.

Lot 20, 120 Montezuma Street, where the Palace's vibrant saloon and dining area's center section is positioned today, has a unique pre–Great Fire history. When the Cabinet and Palace became near neighbors in 1886—separated by lot 20—both used the separating lot, usually halved by a north–south partition. Tonsorial parlors, bathhouses and extra dining space were some of lot 20's functions.

The interior of the Cabinet Saloon after it was rebuilt by D.C. Thorne in 1886. *From Sharlot Hall Museum.*

The Cabinet and Palace Saloons (two doors north of the Cabinet) were separated by lot 20, a bathhouse when this photograph was taken. *From Sharlot Hall Museum.*

In the 1890s, instead of being the shame of Prescott like they were in the 1860s and early '70s, saloons were now an integral and even bragged-about part of Prescott's life and economy.

The temperance movement was gaining momentum throughout the United States, and Prescott was not immune to it. But Whiskey Row survived and even thrived through it all. Some gallant female Salvation Army missionaries did their best to infiltrate and reform the heart of Whiskey Row, or at least the hearts of its devotees. By 1894, these soldiers of sobriety gave up and moved to other towns where success was more likely.

Three years before this, a hotel went up where the Diana Saloon had operated for fifteen years.

THE FUTURE HOTEL ST. MICHAEL BEGINS AS HOTEL BURKE

In 1891, the second Whiskey Row establishment still present today (in a different form, of course) was erected on the southwest corner of Montezuma and Gurley Streets. It was the Hotel Burke at the time. Today it is Hotel St. Michael, with Bistro St. Michael attached. Bistro St. Michael is promoted today with the assertion that "Whiskey Row starts at the bistro."

As detailed earlier, the Diana Saloon was dynamited to the ground during the Whiskey Row fire of 1883. In its place arose the Little Diana, a tiny saloon compared to its predecessor. It stayed on that corner until 1891, when perhaps Prescott's finest pre-1900 structure was thrown into the Whiskey Row lineup.

Dennis Burke and Michael Hickey had in mind a hotel that would eclipse all other efforts at hoteldom in Prescott's pre–Great Fire history. The diminutive Dennis Burke had been a soldier stationed at Fort Whipple as an accountant and chief clerk. He had a gift for numbers and organization. He was discharged with the rank of private but with a character rating of "excellent." Burke wanted to go into business for himself.

Michael Hickey came to America from Ireland via New York City as a twelve-year old. Five years later, gold fever struck him, like it did to so many other young men. He headed to California when the well-known rush was in its latter days. Like so many who did not fare well in California, Hickey headed to the mineral fields of Arizona in 1879. His first stint was in Tombstone, working for a year at the Grand Silver Mine before heading north to the Tiptop Mine in Black Canyon, where he worked and prospected for four years. In 1883, Hickey arrived in Prescott and immediately won over its citizens with his personality. Over the years, he was appointed deputy sheriff three separate times and assisted in many arrests.

Sometime before 1890, Burke and Hickey partnered up and bought two lots on the southwest corner of Montezuma and Gurley Streets. There was a silent third partner, Buckey O'Neill, perhaps Prescott's most revered historical citizen. O'Neill would sell his one-third interest of the hotel to Burke and Hickey in 1894.

Samuel Eason Patton, a Pennsylvanian who moved to Phoenix in 1879, was commissioned to draw up plans for a two-story, forty-two-room hotel with an eye-catching turret. Patton had experienced success in Phoenix, designing the Maricopa County Courthouse and the Maricopa County Hospital, both considered to possess some of the finest architecture in the territory.

The *Courier* urged Burke and Hickey to name their big hotel project "The Goodwin" after Arizona Territory's first governor, John Goodwin. That was a no-go.

In total, the hotel cost them $40,000. They decided to call it Hotel Burke. With great festivity, it opened on New Year's Day in 1891, with a $2 charge

Samuel Eason Patton designed the magnificent Hotel Burke. *From Sharlot Hall Museum.*

for a grand ball and supper. A throng observed the Burke's fine furniture, its first-rate billiard hall, convenient commercial sample rooms and large, elegant dining room. The lobby was so handsome that it soon became the venue for many weddings. For the fellows (and a few nonconformist women), fine cigars and liquors were on hand. Hotel Burke even had a night watchman, tantamount today to a security guard.

Even though they only charged $2.50 to $3.00 a day (a modest $80.00 in today's money), Burke and Hickey felt their resort was unsurpassed by any hotel west of the Mississippi. They were not the only ones. Hotel Burke became the pride of Prescott.

An incident at the hotel in late June 1891, however, gave Prescottonians a reason to raise their eyebrows. On July 1, the *Miner* reported a scandalous story: "Quite a lively scene was enacted around the Hotel Burke Saturday night when Ex-Chief Justice Wright, threatened to kill Adjutant General Gill. As Gill started to walk back to the rear of the room to sit down, Wright attempted to draw his revolver, but was prevented by a bystander. Finally, Sheriff Lowry disarmed the judge, but he continued his abusive language until he was arrested and taken to jail, where he remained all that night." This ex-chief justice in jail had tongues wagging in Prescott. Wright's grievance was never revealed to the public, and he was only charged with carrying concealed weapons.

Hotel Burke soon became *the* place for outsiders to stay in Prescott. It attracted Arizona celebrities—some political and some belonging to theatrical groups. Magnates of mining and cattle ranching often transacted business at the Burke. Easterners claimed that no finer hotel existed in their homelands.

One Hotel Burke guest was the famous "Silver-Orator of the Pacific," Thomas Fitch. It was Fitch who had defended the Earps and Doc Holliday after the now world-famous shootout at the OK Corral in Tombstone. In 1896, Fitch stayed at the Hotel Burke when he was in town to give a speech in support of the Republican candidate for president, William McKinley, on October 15. The speech was said to be stirring.

It is also claimed that Theodore Roosevelt roomed at the Hotel Burke. Sadly, the great man never actually made it to Prescott, although it has been assumed for decades that he had, and the thought has been engraved on a historical plaque and written about in articles and reports.

The Hotel Burke proved such a success that in late 1894—again by the design of Samuel Patton—a thirteen-foot-high third floor was added with twenty-three rooms; in total, the hotel now had sixty-five well-ventilated rooms. It was said that the splendid mountainous and forested landscape surrounding Prescott could be seen from every window for miles. Additionally, its exterior was redone in ornate fashion. Even the impressive corner turret was improved upon—it extended past the third floor and was given an attractive concave piece to add to an ornate French mansard roof.

The interior of the Burke was upgraded in several ways. Doors of the renowned Eastlake design with redwood trim were added to connect the rooms, all of which could house an ordinary-sized family. Now families could rent any number of rooms and not be separated. A large bar—important to the Whiskey Row way of life—was added to the billiard hall. A new 1,720-square-foot kitchen was appended. Perhaps the most significant improvement was that the entire building was no longer lighted by gas but by electricity.

Burke and Hickey were not done yet. A few months later, they laid a sidewalk in front of the hotel. It was composed of red sandstone and was seventy feet long and twelve feet wide. The *Miner* believed that this unique sidewalk "being of a rich color will add still further to the beauty and appearance of the new hotel."

With so much patronage, some comical incidents were bound to occur. On June 26, 1894, an alarm of fire was sounded because smoke was seen emitting from a window. It turned out that a lodger was enjoying his cigars so much that when an ample volume of smoke rolled out of the window, someone walking the street below thought that the room was on fire.

During the last day of July of that same year, a violent incident found its way to Hotel Burke. Dan Flaherty, a prize fighter, had previously had some trouble with Philip Owens—a small man not weighing much more than one hundred pounds. The two had gotten into an argument, which led to Flaherty punching Owens. Owens then pulled his gun, only to be relieved of it.

The little man then grabbed his knife and went after Flaherty with the intention of carving him up. Again, he was somehow disarmed. Owens was subsequently arrested and sentenced to ten days in jail. On the same day Owens was released, he began hunting Flaherty, seeking revenge and to finish what he started. He (who had been stewing in prison) found the pugilist around midnight, enjoying a drink in a Whiskey Row saloon. Owens asked Flaherty if he was armed while reaching for his own weapon. Flaherty was not armed, and he did not wish to be harmed. So, he made a run for it toward the rear exit. Owens took his first shot at the boxer but missed, then followed at a run. The chase was on up Whiskey Row Alley.

Flaherty was not only a good puncher but also a fast runner. Owens struggled to keep up while pulling the trigger several times. Flaherty was heard yelling "murder" and "stop him." Three or four bystanders were nearly hit by stray bullets. One grazed Flaherty's hand.

Upon reaching the Burke, he ran inside hoping for cover. Owens followed Flaherty into the hotel. He had run out of bullets, so Flaherty turned and began grappling with him. Owens had already pulled his knife, again with murderous intent. By now, others had come to Flaherty's aid, including Hotel Burke's night watchman, Joseph McAvin. McAvin was able to wrestle away the knife but not before being cut. Prescottonians were indignant at both Owens and Flaherty, but only Owens was arrested and sentenced to more jail time.

One week before this violent episode, hotel owner Dennis Burke was teased in a *Miner* report because he had finally "succeeded in taming a bicycle." During his first attempt, he was able to ride it around the plaza three times. His goal, however, was seven rounds.

The Hotel Burke also began accepting other businesses into its complex and formed a sort of miniature shopping mall, perhaps a precursor to today's St. Michael's Alley. Harry Brisley, a pharmacist and prominent citizen who would become a key eyewitness to the Great Fire, opened the Mountain City Drugstore inside the Burke. There was also a barbershop and a saloon with a billiard table.

On February 7, 1895, around 2:30 a.m., a fire broke out in the southwest corner of the basement. It was believed to have started in a rat's nest inside a red shirt that had been left behind. Demonstrating how journalism could add a little levity to a situation in those days and get away with it, the *Courier* reported, "It is supposed the rats carried matches to the nest and ignited them by nibbling the ends." Whether or not this was true, this fire was no laughing matter.

The night watchman, McAvin, gave alarm of the fire by discharging his pistol. This woke the guests, who sprang from their beds and hurried to the streets. Also attached to the Burke was a jewelry store. Mr. Lemon, the astute owner, stood by the store door and allowed only police and firefighters in.

Smoke soon filled the hotel's rooms. The fire headed toward Brisley's drugstore, which housed flammable liquors and medicine, but the gallant firemen tamed the fire before it could cause an explosion.

Three years later, in 1898, Herman Voge began his long history with Whiskey Row when he opened a liquor establishment in the Hotel Burke basement—the same place this fire broke out.

In February 1899, Hotel Burke began to publish an advertisement in the *Courier* that would run continuously for a year and a half. In two ways, this ad would come back to haunt Burke and Hickey. First, it bragged that it "employs none but white help in the kitchen"—a sign that racism not only lingered in the territory but was often heralded, promoted and viewed as a positive. Second, it bragged that the Burke was "the only absolutely fireproof hotel in Prescott."

That ad was still running on July 14, 1900.

NEW PROPRIETORS OF THE CABINET SALOON

The 1890s saw new proprietors at the popular Cabinet Saloon—Ben Belcher and Barney Smith. Benjamin Belcher was born on a farm on June 29, 1855, in Farmington, Maine. The Belchers were one of the oldest families in that state. His father was a noted judge who at one time served on the Maine Supreme Court. In 1877, Belcher arrived in Tip Top, Arizona—now a ghost town—where he engaged in general merchandising. Mining eventually became his focus, and he owned several mines, including the well-known Great Belcher Mine.

After moving to Prescott sometime around 1882, Belcher served as a councilman for six years and treasurer of the Elks Lodge for fourteen consecutive years. Before taking co-proprietorship of the Cabinet Saloon, he served as its bartender, a job he began on May 23, 1888. The *Miner* told his visiting "country friends" that they could find their buddy at the Cabinet. He became a co-proprietor in 1891.

Barney Smith was added to the partnership in 1892. Smith was already familiar with the saloon business, having owned the Plaza Bit Saloon on Montezuma Street as far back as the 1870s. The Plaza Bit featured Prescott's first bowling alley. Smith would become another of Prescott's colorful and influential figures and would operate one saloon or another longer, by far, than any other proprietor along Whiskey Row.

Senator Barry Goldwater, whose dream it had been to one day own the Palace Saloon, shared a fond memory of Barney Smith and his wife, Nellie:

Barney Smith in his eighties. Smith holds the record for years spent as a Whiskey Row proprietor. *From Sharlot Hall Museum.*

I always can remember old man Smith would go to work at eight in the morning, walk behind the bar, grab any bottle at hand and start the day's drinking. Around four his wife, a very large woman who taught piano, would come in and play and drink beer. The two of them would wobble out and go home about six. I am told all he ever ate was raw hamburger and he lived to be one heck of an old age, so I am taking up raw hamburger with my bourbon.

On April 7, 1896, after a series of dissolutions with co-proprietors, Belcher and Smith became the only owners of the Cabinet Saloon and would remain so until the Great Fire. After the fire they entered into an even more historic partnership when they joined Bob Brow (now sole proprietor of the Palace) in a grander endeavor.

THE ROUGH RIDERS AND WHISKEY ROW

The 1890s featured much drama along Whiskey Row. The Spanish-American War brought tremendous excitement to Prescott and especially Whiskey Row in 1898. President William McKinley had decided that America should intervene in Cuba's struggle for independence from Spain. Buckey O'Neill—a Whiskey Row regular and Prescott mayor—was not about to allow a chance to fight in a war and represent Arizona Territory and the United States to slip by.

Undersecretary of the navy Theodore Roosevelt conveived of the idea to enlist frontier-toughened men in Arizona, New Mexico, Texas and Oklahoma. Presidential permission was swiftly given to raise this unique regiment. Buckey was its first volunteer. Governor Myron McCord appointed him captain of one of its troops. Soon, Buckey was recruiting qualified men—cowboys and miners and such between eighteen and forty-five years old—on Prescott's plaza from Prescott, Yavapai County and other parts of Arizona.

With all these men prone to living the Wild West way of life in town, Whiskey Row suddenly became more popular, and rowdier. It is rumored that some recruits visited every saloon—some say there were forty saloons in all, but that is probably a high estimation—in one day before heading off to San Antonio to train for war.

The Palace Saloon was a favorite of those who would soon be known as the Rough Riders. Bob Brow was an especially fervent supporter of the volunteers. He even donated a troop mascot—a mountain lion named Florence. During the war, Brow kept Palace patrons up to date regarding how "Teddy's Terrors" were doing. He hired an artist who—strikingly and very realistically, read one report—illustrated their actions during their training, deployment and eventually battles on blackboard. This consistently drew sizable crowds.

The send-off given to these soldiers was perhaps Prescott's grandest event to date. The troopers marched up Montezuma Street and were surrounded by the sight of waving handkerchiefs, flags and encouraging shouts. They arrived at the train depot on Sheldon Street and boarded four Santa Fe, Prescott and Phoenix railroad cars. As they set out for Texas, Prescottonians heartily serenaded them with "God Be with You Till We Meet Again."

It would be the final time Buckey O'Neill would see Prescott and his beloved Whiskey Row. As O'Neill was shouting out commands just before the Rough Riders made their famous charges up Kettle and San Juan Hills, a Spanish bullet, of which he had just moments before said to a sergeant that there was not one "made that will kill me," ended his life. Colonel Roosevelt

The bronze statue honoring Buckey O'Neill and the Rough Riders before its unveiling. *From Nancy Burgess.*

Solon Borglum's bronze equestrian statue pays homage to Buckey O'Neill and the Rough Riders. *From Nancy Burgess.*

wrote, "As he turned on his heel a bullet struck him in the mouth and came out at the back of his head, so that even before he fell his wild and gallant soul had gone out into the darkness."

In 1905, the renowned sculptor Solon Borglum—brother of Gutzon Borglum, the sculptor of Mount Rushmore—was commissioned to create a bronze statue that would commemorate Buckey and the Rough Riders. On July 3, seven thousand people gathered around the shrouded monument after a mile-long parade that included some Rough Riders. Cheers erupted when Buckey's stepson, Maurice, pulled the ropes and unveiled one of Borglum's best works: a cowboy-looking soldier reining in a rearing stallion. It still stands as one of the top attractions in downtown Prescott and one of the finest equestrian statues in the world.

As the nineteenth century was coming to a close, life was relatively uneventful in Prescott and along Whiskey Row. The main concern for many was a dwindling supply of water due to an extended drought and the absence of a suitable waterworks system. Fire was a constant concern. A few even realized that an all-consuming conflagration was possible. The year 1900 would not remain uneventful in this frontier town. Prescott and its Whiskey Row were about to suddenly and drastically change.

6

PRELUDE TO A CONFLAGRATION, 1900

Hot.
No water.
Getting Hotter.
Cisterns all dry.
Bad time to have a fire.
—Arizona Weekly Journal-Miner

The above quote was a perfect description of Prescott weather and its water supply conditions on July 14, 1900. But it came from a *Miner* blurb on June 6, 1879, not 1900. It could have been written during many pre-1900 springs and summers.

The year 1900 in the United States found William McKinley serving as president. He was nearing the tail-end of his first four years, and his re-election campaign was underway. After Theodore Roosevelt's heroics in Cuba during the Spanish-American War, his political career rocketed. Roosevelt was now McKinley's running mate and was beloved in Prescott.

This did not stop the Democrats' presidential nominee, William Jennings Bryan, from making a campaign stop in Prescott in 1900. The celebrated orator, who had stumped in Prescott for the same reason four years earlier, visited in mid-April during a train tour through the West. Prescottonians called the event "Bryan Day." Bryan gave his speech in front of the courthouse, near where the Buckey O'Neill/Rough Rider statue stands today.

Not unlike modern political campaign speeches, it was alleged that Bryan's oration was mostly a harangue against the opposing party, not a platform of new ideas. It was common for people who attended Bryan rallies to pay more attention to his oratorical skills than the content of his addresses. For that reason, he drew big crowds. Many Prescottonians proved immune to his charms, though Bryan supporters viewed the event as a rousing success.

There was a hangover effect to hosting a presidential candidate event. The "Bryan blowout" was costly. For that reason, a majority of Prescott businessmen thought it best to not have a Fourth of July celebration in 1900. There was also the matter of a Rough Riders' reunion that was promised to be held in Prescott in 1901. Time, energy and money, it was argued, might be better used for that. Prescott did not want to disappoint because maybe Theodore Roosevelt would show, and most likely as the vice president of United States. The McKinley/Roosevelt ticket was expected to win in November.

In lieu of a Fourth of July celebration, the *Howler*—Prescott's third newspaper, described as "racy society journal" by the *Tombstone Prospector*—suggested that a Prescott tug-of-war team should be sent to Jerome during their celebration "to show denizens of the copper town a thing or two about that popular and muscular sport."

There was an ideological struggle in 1900 between Americans who were concerned that their still relatively new country was expanding too quickly—that it was too greedy and ambitious—and adversative idealists who believed that all-out American imperialism would only improve the world.

The latter thought was best expressed in an oft-used McKinley/Roosevelt campaign slogan: "The American flag has not been planted in foreign soil to acquire more territory but for humanity's sake." This statement was an apologetic for the Spanish-American War, just won by the Americans, and was credited to President McKinley. It was voiced on July 12, 1900, two days before disaster struck Whiskey Row. To many Arizonans, this declaration raised hopes for statehood.

A big chunk of what are now the forty-eight contiguous states of America was missing in 1900. The present states of Arizona and New Mexico, then divided into two sizable territories, formed a bridge between California and the United States' new Midwest but were still not states. They were mere territories. Territorial tutelage was usually short, but it had not been so for the rough-edged Arizona Territory.

Prescott was at the center of the statehood issue. Although Phoenix was growing exponentially and was now the territorial capital, Prescott was still considered by many to be the heart of Arizona. Indeed, it was important enough to attract a presidential candidate hoping to earn Arizona's favor.

Four months before the Great Fire, long-distance telephoning had been established between Prescott and Phoenix. The *Miner* reporter present during this historic occasion was astonished, as anyone with proper sensibilities would have been in 1900, that "their voices were easily recognizable and their articulation could be heard as distinctly as though they were standing only a few feet [from] the person addressing them instead of being over 100 miles away."

The local newspapers, especially the *Miner* and *Courier*, were hitting Prescottonians day after day with advertisements offering solutions to multifarious health problems. They were often masked as actual reports. A headline was followed by so-called breaking news. The elixir salesman, aided by the local pharmacist, was foremost among those practicing this mountebankery. One of the most attention-grabbing advertisements proffered a tonic called "Nervita," said to cure "impotency, night emissions and wasting diseases, all effects of self-abuse, or excess and indiscretion."

Another bold enterprise marketed an elixir called "S.S.S for the Blood." In separate issues of the *Miner*, this concoction of vegetable juices was said to cure little pimples that turn to cancer (February 7); rheumatism (February 28); scrofula and consumption (March 7); eczema, also called the "satanic itch" by its sellers (March 14); sores and ulcers (April 4); and blood poisoning (April 17).

Most advertisements included the testimony of somebody somewhere said to occupy a prominent place in society, a successful person, or at the very least somebody who could not be charged with being unintelligent or unimportant and could not possibly be lying.

One ad, brazen to the point of being outright offensive, cautioned women that they had "no right to ugliness," stating, "The woman who is lovely in face, form and temper will always have friends, but one who would be attractive must keep her health." The remedy? Just run over to one of the two Harry Brisley's drugstores and ante up fifty cents for some "Electric Bitters," a medicine that could cure "a wretched complexion" caused by impure blood due to constipation and/or urinary issues. So powerful was this inexpensive medication that it could "make a good-looking, charming woman of a run-down invalid."

Times were mostly good in Prescott in 1900. There was a relative calm and prosperity. There were signs of even better times ahead. Hotel Burke had extended south and had taken in the Owl Saloon as part of its complex.

This was viewed as a sign of progress—it "argues well for a prosperous year," said the *Miner*. There was a new saloon/resort on Gurley Street called the Comet. Quality saloons in Prescott were the indicators of the mountain town's prosperity.

The mining industry was performing at full strength in the surrounding Bradshaw Mountains. Prosperity was still the reality and promise of the day. Although a plethora of reports came out after the Great Fire alleging that Prescott was stagnant, the *Courier* claimed that the town was growing: "The surest criterion by which to judge the growth and increasing population of Prescott is the activity noticeable in the leading business houses of Prescott."

Sam Hill's Hardware—from which the phrase "what in the Sam Hill?" has been falsely declared to have originated—was flourishing. Something akin to the well-known saying might have been uttered a time or two or more, though. It is said that Sam Hill's had such a wide selection of items that covered three lots that one, indeed, had cause to ask, "What in the Sam Hill is that?!"

Times were good in Prescott, but anyone who has lived in Arizona knows that eventually two topics are bound to come up: heat and drought. Even in the highlands in which Prescott is sited. In the early summer of 1900, these two subjects were more than just talk. As detailed earlier, when summer tiptoes into the central highlands and forests of Arizona, dry spells come with it. In 1900, several years of drought preceded summer. Water was obviously needed for drinking, plumbing, irrigation and watering plants and animals. It was also needed to—if the situation arose—extinguish fires. There was no surplus of this precious element available in Prescott in 1900.

So desperate was the concern about this drought that Prescott's mayor pro tempore Fred Brecht (Mayor John Dougherty was out of town "as usual," one pioneer woman averred) issued an emergency edict in the *Miner* and *Courier*. It was a "notice to [the] water consumers" of Prescott on May 21, 1900. It was published up until July 14 and even a few days after.

A ban was enacted regarding the watering of lawns and gardens. Realizing there was still a need for this, an exception was made in the evening hours between seven and eight o'clock. The chief of police, Steve Prince, was instructed not only to inform every household of this measure but also to report individuals violating the injunction. The punishment for any violations was the loss of water privileges altogether.

Some Great Fire narratives claim that Prescott was still composed of nothing but wood buildings in 1900. However, brick structures were more common in Prescott and along Whiskey Row than in the past. Wood was still the most prominent component for most false-fronted structures. There was an odd combination of flammable and non-flammable.

But wood was only part of the problem in the late spring and early summer of 1900. The middle of June found Mayor John Dougherty back in town. Early on he visited his brother Joe, owner of the OK Grocery Store located on the northwest corner of Gurley and Granite Streets. During this visit, an argument between the brothers was overheard by an employee, Bert Lee.

Joe was not pleased that his mayor/brother and the Prescott City Council seemed more concerned about the town's physical appearance than its physical safety. Ironically, an unusually wet early winter (followed by a completely dry middle and late winter and spring) had left the streets of Prescott in a rutted condition. A decision had been made by the mayor and the city council to spend available funds to grade the streets rather than finding a way to increase Prescott's water supply and delivery.

Joe argued, "Why the hell do you have to grade the streets right now? If you're short of money, what you got ought to do is deepen those wells or dig new ones. What if we have a fire—how'd you stop it?" Neither could have realized how prophetic those words would prove a month later.

The streets of Prescott were rutted in 1900 due to an unusually wet early winter. Note Sam Hill's Hardware where many explosive materials were stored. *From Nancy Burgess.*

In the OK Grocery Store, the Dougherty brothers argued about whether paving Prescott's rutted streets should have precedence over improving the town's water supply. *From Sharlot Hall Museum.*

The mayor fired back that there was enough water to handle whatever problems might arise, and besides, the people of Prescott wanted those streets graded before anything else.

The grocery man was incredulous. He pointed at Lee and shouted, "Ask Bert here. He'll tell you there isn't enough water to put out a chicken coop if it was on fire." Indeed, water was at a premium. Prescottonians were surely aware that if a fire was to break out now, it would be extremely difficult to extinguish. Or were they convinced that if a conflagration had not happened by now, it never would?

Waterworks had been a much talked about and debated issue since Prescott's inception and was still a hot topic in 1900. Exactly one month before the Great Fire—shortly after this telling incident between the Dougherty brothers—the *Courier* printed a statement that now reads like a loud I told you so. It stated, "The *Courier* has advocated the putting of a windmill over the southwest well of the plaza for some years." Had those in charge listened to the local media, the history of Prescott and Whiskey Row might have emerged in an entirely different manner.

The southwest corner of the plaza would become a focal point of hope on that starry but hot and dry night of July 14, 1900.

On July 3, Mayor Dougherty's decision to pave the streets provided the locals an inadvertent dash of hope. The *Miner* noted, "There was a slight sprinkle that occurred up and down Montezuma street yesterday afternoon, but it came from Arizona Paving Co.'s water cart."

The ironies of cause had reached a crescendo. A multitude of factors for an urban fire-borne catastrophe were in place.

Such was the situation in Prescott on July 14, 1900. But life went on as usual in the saloon town. It was said, in fact, that life was going on more vigorously than usual, that an unusually fluid flow of libations was running on that hot summer night. Famous Prescottonian George Ruffner has been often reported to have uttered, "To jail all drunks in Prescott tonight you'd have to put a roof over the town." Ruffner was not the Yavapai County sheriff at the time of the Great Fire, although it has been assumed that he was. Is this claim true? It cannot be known.

Miners, cowboys, sportsmen and soldiers were hitting the noisy and crowded saloons, leaning against the bars, slaking their thirst by enjoying a nickel beer or a whiskey or maybe some fancy drink if they had no shame. And if not a fancy drink in their hands, they were negotiating terms with a fancy lady. Cigars were providing the ambient incense. Roulette wheels were whirring. Faro dealers were shouting out their calls. Ragtime pianists were banging out lively tunes, reflecting the general mood of the night. Due to high temperatures, Harry Brisley's Mountain City Drug Store was doing exceptional business with its soda fountain. Ice cream was also a particularly popular item there. And, yes, the bawdy houses on Granite Street were doing a resounding business.

But this semi-controlled chaos would soon pale in comparison.

7

DECIPHERING THE CAUSE

Historic events of great magnitude generate dispute, disagreement and controversy. Essential details are often initially missing because in the hurry to find them, what often transpires is well-intentioned but erroneous information. Later, the historian must sift through everything that has been written and said, then make deductions as to what is true and what is false, or what is likely. Newspaper reports, the first drafts of history at that time, created frequent problems with early accounts, just like today when a television news station rushes to report the details of a tragic event. Furthermore, such events are often shrouded in chaos, both before the event and after.

These circumstances make getting to the root cause a challenge. The Great Fire of 1900 is no exception. The biggest difficulty in deciphering and piecing together a narrative for the Great Fire of 1900 derives from the fact that the headquarters for Prescott's key newspapers, the *Miner* and the *Courier*, burned down. Both hurried to get up and running again, but there was little time to go on fact-finding missions. Moreover, hearsay was running rampant.

When these newspapers returned to publishing the news, the primary focus of the first reports was not describing the fire itself but the status of Prescott in general and the many businesses the fire destroyed. There was the critical question of whether proprietors, like themselves, planned to rebuild and, if so, where they would locate their temporary quarters. Would the dream that was Prescott continue, or would they haul down their banners, surrender and move on after such sudden and complete destruction? The answer depended on what business owners planned to do after the loss of their establishments. Everyone was eager to know.

The question was answered with a resounding, "Yes! Prescott will push on and rebuild something better!" Business owners were urgently looking ahead, not back. Consequently, there was little effort to recount what had happened during the inferno, let alone investigate the cause of the fire. They were recovering from the disaster and scrambling to get back in business. Although townsfolk put on a happy face, they understandably were still in shock from seeing the heart of their town wiped out.

There was also the inability to report on the many heroic, colorful, even bizarre stories caused by the desperation of Prescott's crowded hour. The *Courier* shed some light on the situation on July 19 by admitting, "There is no space in this paper to give in detail the deeds of daring done to save a neighbor's property which were witnessed on this eventful occasion."

These stories would not immediately become known to the public. Instead, they surfaced over years and even decades, primarily during reunions occurring long after the catastrophe, usually in intervals of five or ten years throughout the early and mid-1900s, when those who helped fight the fire and/or those who witnessed the Great Fire would gather on July 14 to reminisce and share their experiences. These storytelling anniversaries transpired in Prescott as far out as seventy-five years after the fact.

When discussing the cause of the fire, even to this day there is still the occasional "I heard that…" Some say it is a mystery and always will be. Certainly no one was about to take "credit" for starting the tragedy. It has been thought that there were no eyewitnesses to the cause, but there is evidence to the contrary. And there is more than enough testimony to reach a strong conclusion.

One commonly told account regarding the origins of the Great Fire has a drunken miner accidentally kicking over a lantern inside a building. This theory, coming out of nowhere like Mrs. O'Leary's cow of the Great Chicago Fire of 1871, somehow gained legs over time, even after another theory had already been generally accepted. It has proven to be only legend with no evidence backing it up.

Two of the earliest reports came from the *Arizona Republican* out of Phoenix and the *Los Angeles Herald*. These newspapers claimed that the "fire started in a room over J.E. Burchard's Bottling Works on South Montezuma Street where a man is said to have been lying in bed reading a paper. In some

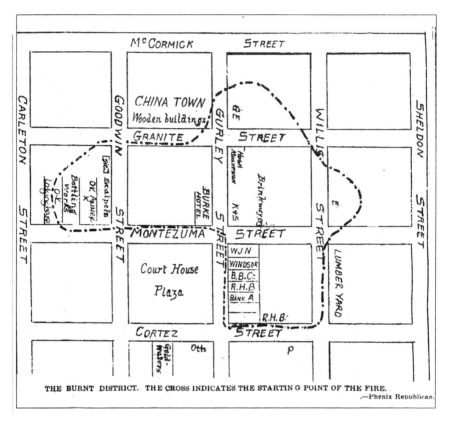

THE BURNT DISTRICT. THE CROSS INDICATES THE STARTING POINT OF THE FIRE.
—Phènix Republican.

The map that was used on July 19, 1900, to show the Great Fire's path contains three errors, all delineated on this page and the following. *From Bradley G. Courtney.*

manner the paper on the wall took fire and instead of the man attempting to extinguish it he ran out and gave an alarm of fire."

The *Arizona Republican* received its information via desperate telegraphs first sent to Jerome, which initially got its information from Prescott's Western Union office located in the Hotel Burke. There, the operator frantically tapped out reports before vacating to Goldwater's Store on Cortez Street. In the confusion and haste, inaccurate information was disseminated.

On July 19, the *Arizona Republican* published a map showing that Burchard's Bottling Works was part of the Scopel Block on the west side of Montezuma Street, just south of Goodwin Street between the southward OK Lodging House and the northward OK Annex. The *Miner* also issued the map on July 19 even though it originated from the *Arizona Republican*. It contained at least three errors, one of which is the location of Burchard's

Bottling Works. The other two errors are that the fire crossed Granite and Willis Streets. It did not.

The accompanying report stated that a man who had been outside Burchard's Bottling Works filled a bucket using a nearby faucet. He ran upstairs to the room and attempted to douse the flame. Needing more water, the man hurried back to the faucet, where he found such insubstantial pressure that it took much longer to refill the bucket. He gave up in disgust. Evidence points to the likelihood that this report is at least partially true. There is even more evidence that a man ran out of a building shooting a gun into the air warning Prescott residents that there was a fire, but it was not from the Burchard's building.

The claim that the fire's origin was in Burchard's Bottling Works, said to have had two stories in the July 19 *Arizona Republican* report, is easily disproven. An image of the building between the OK Lodging House and the OK Annex—where Burchard's was mapped out to be—shows that it was a one-story house with no upstairs for anyone to be in. More importantly—thanks to the *Mojave County Miner*, which caught the mistake—it was noted that there was a Burchard's Bottling Works in Prescott, but it was not located in the Scopel Block. It sat one street west on Granite Street. Burchard's was clearly an early victim of the fire, but it was not where the fire began.

Another common belief, also easily debunked, is that Whiskey Row's big fire began in the "Scopel Hotel" or "Scopel House," which was actually called the Grandview House. Ferdinand Scopel, an Italian, was the namesake and owner of a block of businesses—the Scopel Block—which included, from south to north, the OK Lodging House, the OK Annex, the Humphries and Davison Commission Merchants, a repair shop, Alfred Avery's Grocery Store and the Grandview House.

The beautifully bricked, stately Grandview House stood tall and narrow on the southwest corner of Montezuma and Goodwin Streets. Because the Great Fire began in the Scopel Block, in many retellings over the decades, it has been inaccurately changed to the Scopel Hotel.

A preponderance of evidence leads to a clear conclusion: The Whiskey Row Fire of 1900 started in the OK Lodging House—sometimes called the Miner's Lodging House by locals—at the southern end of the Scopel Block. One or more miners were the culprit, and a miner's candlestick holder is at the center of the Great Fire's origin.

Right: Italian Ferdinand Scopel owned the Scopel Block, which included the Grandview House, the OK Annex and the OK Lodging House. *From Sharlot Hall Museum.*

Below: The Great Fire began in the OK Lodging House of the Scopel Block. The Grandview House sat on the corner of Montezuma and Goodwin Streets. *From Sharlot Hall Museum.*

ERWIN BAER, Photographer.   PRESCOTT, ARIZONA.

THE MINER'S CANDLESTICK HOLDER

One theme has endured over the decades regarding the cause of the Great Fire of 1900: a mine worker's misuse of a miner's candlestick holder. There are several versions of it. But first, a short description and history of the miner's candlestick holder is in order.

A miner's candlestick holder was an inexpensive device used to provide light in mines. Usually made of cast iron, it had a spike that could either be driven into an apposite crack in the mine wall or into the mine's sturdy framing timber. A candle could be inserted and clamped to a thimble of sorts on the side. Miner's candlestick holders were carried by miners much like those working in darker places today might carry a flashlight. A miner was not usually given a candlestick holder by the company he worked for—he was responsible for purchasing and carrying his own. He often kept it with him wherever he went, even to hotels and lodging houses.

In the 1900s, such places were often without carbide or electric lamps, especially along the western frontier. The temptation to jab a miner's candlestick holder into a lodging house wall is understandable, but obviously, they were not designed to be stuck into walls that were made of wood and surrounded by flammable material.

Some candlestick holders sported a mechanism that snuffed out the candle when it neared the end of the tallow. However, miners did not appreciate these holders because they extinguished the little flame before the workers in the mines were prepared, causing them to suddenly find themselves in complete darkness. Miners would rather let the candle drop to the floor as a warning that a new candle was needed.

As will be seen, a candlestick holder with a snuffing mechanism would have come in handy on July 14, 1900. But they fell out of fashion long before.

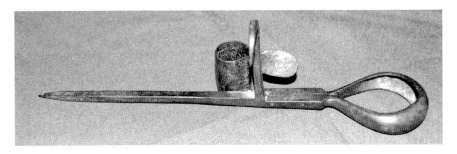

A fallen candle from a miner's candlestick holder started the spark that led to a conflagration in Prescott on July 14, 1900. *From John McKinney and Norman Fisk.*

FIRE IN THE OK LODGING HOUSE

As mentioned, Burchard's Bottling Works was initially named as the starting point of the fire. That rumor spread almost as fast as the fire itself. Within days, however, the story began changing, and the truth was unveiled.

On July 16, the aforementioned *Howler*, an upstart semiweekly local newspaper that was more akin to a gossip rag—according to some locals, "a bear-cat on wheels"—published Prescott's first report of the Great Fire. It also was the first to mention that a miner's negligent use of his candlestick holder in a lodging house was the probable cause of the fire that wiped out Prescott's economic center.

The *Howler* stated:

> *The fire started in the rooming house* [the OK Lodging House] *just south of the Scopel block at 10:30 Saturday night. It is said to have originated in one of the rooms through the carelessness of a miner, who had placed a miner's candlestick* [holder] *with a candle stuck into the wall, while he went out into the street. The candle fell through on the floor and ignited the carpet. Another report current, that a lamp exploded and set the rooming house afire, but the candle version is generally accepted as the right one.*

More than one Prescott historian names the accused miner as Ed Harrold. Although Harrold played a part in the Great Fire, he was not the man who jabbed a candlestick holder into a rooming house wall. Harrold's story is told in chapter 12.

The most definitive proof that the negligent use of a miner's candlestick holder caused the Great Fire came from Ferdinand Scopel himself. Only eleven days after the conflagration, on July 26, the *Courier* clearly conveyed the explanation. Interestingly, this was not front-page news but was printed on page 3, and it read more like a side note. Perhaps this revealed the forward-looking mindset of the people of Prescott. Or perhaps the miner's candlestick holder as cause was already being accepted around town. The report read in full:

> *A million and a half dollars* [the estimated loss of property value given soon after the fire] *is a pretty good price to pay for a glass of beer. Nevertheless that is about the price Prescott pays for a glass of beer which a lodger in the Scopel Block drank. Mr. Scopel pointed out to the* Courier

reporter the man who drank his costly drink, and he by no means had the appearance of a man who would insist on high priced articles, as a million and a half dollar drink. Mr. Scopel said the lodger went to his room, lit a candle, put it in a miner's candlestick, stuck it in the wall and went down for a glass of beer; while he was gone the candlestick fell down. The lighted candle ignited the wallpaper.

This excerpt answers the main question regarding cause. But how did the Italian entrepreneur learn of this? A deduction can be made. Almost certainly, there were others in the room who saw this man inserting the candlestick holder into the lodging house wall, but they shifted the blame away from themselves and toward one person. Although there are varying versions of the miner's candlestick holder story as the Great Fire's cause, there is enough evidence to reach reasonable conclusions and provide a most-likely scenario.

At least one miner, looking for a little vacation from the toils of digging for ore, leased a room in the OK Lodging House for one dollar. There were probably four miners in the room, as it was common for workers coming into Prescott to share a room, especially when the fee was as much as a dollar. Twenty-five cents each was more affordable than one dollar; a dollar is equivalent to about thirty dollars in today's currency.

This still may seem cheap, but keep in mind that rooms such as those offered by the OK Lodging House provided little more than beds—perhaps not even clean ones. The conditions of such rooms were often appalling. OK Lodging House rooms were probably of poor quality like most lodging house rooms of that day.

Several narratives state that these miners were Italian. If true, this may have resulted from an inclination to rent a room from a fellow Italian, Ferdinand Scopel.

These men hit Whiskey Row and commenced their plan to drink a lot of booze and enjoy the delights the Row offered. How many saloons they visited, and for how long, is unknown. For whatever reason, they decided at some point to return to their OK Lodging House room. It was dark now, and they needed light in their cheap room. One miner grabbed his candlestick holder and jabbed it into the wooden wall, inserted a candle and lit the wick.

Perhaps the miners had returned intending to stay in for the night and then changed their minds. Regardless, they headed down to the Cellar Saloon, located on the bottom floor of the more upscale Grandview House. None thought to extinguish the candle gently burning in the candleholder.

Jake Weber was also down at the Cellar that night as a customer. He noted that other patrons were drinking more than usual, so much so that at the request of the owner, he and a friend known as Missoury headed over to Jake Marks's liquor store on Gurley Street to buy another keg to satisfy the customers' penchant for alcohol that night.

As the men drank on, the burning candle was not on their minds. It continued to burn until it eventually unclamped and fell onto the bed below.

Several accounts assert that a curtain caught on fire after the wind blew it into the burning candle. Others say the flame simply ignited the wallpaper, or the candle fell and landed on the carpet. However, according to historian Pat Savage, there were two eyewitnesses who saw that a bed was the first to provide fuel for the candle's flamelet. One was the aforementioned Bert Lee of the OK Grocery Store, who also was a volunteer fireman and foreman of the OK Hose Company. His testimony is disclosed in the next chapter.

8

PRESCOTT LEARNS THAT A FIRE HAS STARTED IN THE SCOPEL BLOCK

What was happening when the fire started upstairs in the OK Lodging House and then grew in size?

Ben Powers was sitting outside the lodging house when the fire started. A guest ran out of the building shooting a gun and yelling, "Fire!" Powers yelled back, "Cut it out, man. I know there's a fire, but I didn't start it and I'm not going to get shot for it."

Jake Weber recounted that he and Missoury had just finished their second glasses of beer in the Cellar Saloon when they heard gunshots. Hurrying toward the noise, they learned that someone was alerting the town of a nearby fire.

Charles Ryland, a sign painter, had just retired for the night when he heard those same gunshots. He thought maybe a gunfight was transpiring on Whiskey Row. Running toward where he had heard the sounds, it was not long before he spotted a glow in the sky and realized there was a fire.

Little Belle Campbell was the daughter of John Campbell, one of Prescott's first mercantile store owners and a congressional delegate. According to the *Courier* after one of the Great Fire anniversary gatherings, she was eating watermelon inside her family's house on North Granite Street "when she first heard the sound of fire gongs and rifle and pistol reports that gave the alarm."

One guest of the OK Lodging House saw the first flames and ran out to fill a bucket with water from the nearest faucet. He believed he would be able to easily douse what he had seen. However, not enough water came from the spigot to discover if this was true.

About 10:30 p.m., a steam siren that firemen nicknamed "Old Mockingbird" sounded. Two young brothers, Bill and Jim Fitzgerald, and their buddy Earl Rhodes were camping on the Fitzgerald lawn at 502 South Cortez Street on this warm night. They had been to a Salvation Army ice cream social earlier that evening and were feeling giddy.

The siren, powered by two hundred pounds of steamed pressure, made the three boys sit up and take notice, as it did many other Prescottonians. Bill and Jim's parents ordered them to stay put, but of course, they did not. The mother of the Fitzgerald boys and Earl's mother chased after them toward Whiskey Row. They would all become eyewitnesses to one of the most spectacular urban blazes the West has ever known.

Gail Gardner, who later became a local legend and a well-known cowboy poet, was a small boy in 1900. On July 14, he remembered that his mother had unsuccessfully tried to get water from the kitchen faucet. She casually remarked after hearing the ear-splitting siren, "What a bad night for a fire."

BERT LEE AND THE OK HOSE COMPANY
REACH THE OK LODGING HOUSE

Bert Lee had finished a thirteen-hour workday at the OK Grocery Store; Saturdays were always busy there. Wearily making his way home, he downed his dinner and went to bed. A short time after falling asleep, he heard Old Mockingbird crying out to Prescott. Hastily climbing into his Levi's and boots, he took a quick glance at the clock. It was 10:45 p.m.

Rooming with Lee was another volunteer fireman, Gilbert Taylor. Both sprinted toward the hose house. Along the way, they encountered Johnny Cortum, who rented a house behind Lee's abode. Cortum was not a fireman, but he wanted to help, and Lee was glad to have him. Lee's younger brother, Carl, joined them shortly after.

Running westward along Gurley Street, the three men reached the hose house, which was about 100 feet from the OK Grocery Store. This was also a pump house and was in disrepair. Nearby was a 475-foot-deep well that was completely dry. The men grabbed the hose cart and hurried toward Granite Creek, where it got stuck in the gravel. A man riding horseback nearby tossed the boys a lariat, which they attached to the hose cart. The strength of the horse was all that was needed to free the cart from the creek bed, and the three once again rushed toward the smoke.

A Prescott hose and pump house around the time of the Great Fire. *From Sharlot Hall Museum.*

Soon, other members of the OK Company were running alongside the hose cart and guiding it down Granite Street, then eastward using Goodwin Street toward Montezuma Street. Now working with the Lee brothers were Martin Testori, Charlie Young, Jimmy Morral, Gilbert Taylor, Tom Simmons, Worth Rybon and Phil Hartin. Stopping short of Montezuma, they turned south down the alley behind the Scopel Block and stopped at the rear of the OK Lodging House. Onlookers had begun to gather.

The Lee brothers climbed a set of stairs while the hydrant man, Testori, screwed the hose to the nearest fire hydrant. When the Lees reached the fated room, they saw a bed that was on fire on the far side of the room. Above the bed near a corner was a miner's candlestick holder: "The candle had evidently burned down until it heated the metal ring that held it, then the stub had fallen through and onto the bed," Lee told Savage.

Training the hose on the fire that was now climbing "up the pitchy walls and eating through the roof," a three-foot stream, "the consistency of pancake batter," was all that could be mustered before it became pure mud. After three gallons had passed through the hose, the output dwindled to a dribble.

Bert Lee and the boys gave up hope and joined in fighting the flames by other means. Lee headed up Montezuma Street to help pull out the immense inventory in Sam Hill's Hardware. Sam Hill himself was out of town and unaware that his store was in jeopardy.

WATER IS RELEASED FROM THE RESERVOIR

Harry Brisley, the previously mentioned pharmacist who owned two downtown drugstores that would burn to the ground during Prescott's fiery nightmare, was an eyewitness to most, if not all, of the Great Fire. He wrote of an incident occurring during the earliest stages of the fire.

There "occurred a scene worthy of a Western movie thriller around the corner of Gurley and Cortez streets, hastening from another duty was the city engineer and his familiar wagon, grievously belaboring his old white horse. Thence sharply turning into the corner of Gurley and South Montezuma, they together continued their fevered race toward the reservoir." This heroic figure was John Love, Prescott's city water engineer.

It is important to note that the reservoir was lower than usual but not dry.

Absent from accounts of the Great Fire of 1900 is an astounding revelation that may have been kept quiet for years. According to Bill Fitzgerald, after reaching the reservoir, Love started the pumps and sent ample water to the water mains and hydrants. However, after residents initially received insufficient water from the hydrants and wells, and in their desperation to find other means to fight the fire, the fresh supply went unnoticed. Love stayed at the reservoir for the duration of the fire, awaiting instructions that never came.

THE WELL OF HOPE

The *Miner* reported on September 17, 1880, that the well on the southwest corner of the plaza—at the junction of Goodwin and Montezuma Streets—had just been completed. "It is 45 feet deep, 4 feet in diameter, and has two tunnels 4 x 6 feet wide and high, and each 15 feet in length. The water level is 25 feet from the surface, and the well, when full to that point, holds between 8,000 and 9,000 gallons of water." On July 14, 1900, this would become the well of hope in Prescott after the fire alarm sounded at 10:45 p.m.

After a dry spring and early summer and years of drought, there was little water, not only in that well but also in all four plaza wells situated on each of the plaza's cardinal direction corners. While Bert Lee and the OK Company were attempting to snuff the flames inside the OK Lodging House, two other hose companies, the Toughs and the Dudes, had been on the move and were hooking up to that southwest corner plaza well.

Harry Brisley wrote that a crowd had quickly gathered near that corner, hoping to see the flames quickly extinguished. "A few minutes longer, and the slowly swelling hose proved the pumps were in motion, while anxious observers vividly realized that the city faced the severest hours of its [thirty-six] years' history, when from the nozzle came a dirty stream falling weakly to the street a few feet from the source," he explained. The firemen threw down the hose in consternation and left it in the street.

Firefighters, unaware that John Love had sent water down from the reservoir, believed there was not enough water available in the mains and wells to fight this mounting fire. Probably about the time Love was releasing water from the reservoir, they began their dependence on dynamite, which had worked to save Prescott in the 1883 and 1884 fires. Prescott might be short of water, but as a mining town, it was never at a loss for "giant" or "miner's" powder.

9

DYNAMITING BEGINS AND THE FIRE JUMPS GOODWIN STREET

Ferdinand Scopel's Grandview House, which also housed the *Courier* headquarters, was considered "magnificent" by locals. It featured some of the finest architecture in town. As the house was made of brick, there was hope it could be saved. Therefore, the building bordering the southern wall of the Grandview, the OK Annex, was blown to bits and flattened.

It was for naught. Harry Brisley testified that the fire then "entered" the Grandview House. The firefighters concluded that it, too, would have to be dynamited.

Some questions arise: Did these firefighters have any experience dynamiting brick buildings such as the Grandview House? Surely, they understood the hazards associated with blowing up wooden-frame buildings. But what about buildings constructed of brick? Yes, dynamiting had worked during the fires of 1883 and 1884, but no brick edifices were involved.

The firefighters placed in the "vortex of heat, sufficient dynamite to crumble walls to the earth." Astoundingly, "the masonry stood firm," Brisley wrote. Photographic evidence demonstrates that at least the northern wall of the Grandview House did indeed stand firm.

Because the Grandview House was not only solid but also tall and narrow, it behaved like an enormous cannon. According to Brisley, the embers and sparks and "firey [*sic*] forks" did not blow straight across Goodwin to the Montezuma Street segment of the infamous Block 13, but because of strong winds blowing north and west, they blew toward the buildings on Granite Street.

So far, the rest of Montezuma Street above Goodwin Street had been skipped.

Harry Brisley noted that the Grandview House's "masonry stood firm." Here it can be seen that its north wall did indeed refuse to crumble. *From Sharlot Hall Museum.*

RUMORS NEVER PROVEN OR DISPROVEN

The initial reports out of Phoenix and Los Angeles reported that a man had been killed during the Great Fire, and the story was a doozy. Part of the *Arizona Republican* headlines screamed on July 16, "UNKNOWN MAN PERISHED IN THE RAGING FLAMES."

Before the dynamite was set off in the Grandview House, a man was reported to have been standing somewhere along the edge of the top story of the hotel. Firefighters shouted at the man that the building was about to be blown up and to take advantage of the ladder they were offering him. Instead, "He was then surrounded by flame and only answered with a maniacal laugh. Nothing was seen of him afterward," claimed the *Arizona Republican*. Prescott newspapers later reported that there were no fatalities during the Great Fire.

If this *Arizona Republican* story of a man's death has credence, surely there would have been no trace of the remains of the man given the intensity of the fire. Neither the *Miner*, the *Courier* nor even the *Howler* specifically refuted this claim, and it was never mentioned after the initial report. Whether the first reports were true will never be known, but it certainly is possible.

Fifty years later, Little Belle Morshead, formerly Little Belle Campbell, told the *Courier* that she believed that one man was hit by exploding bullets from a burning building during the Great Fire and later died from those wounds. Mrs. Morshead stated that the man was on the banks of Granite Creek when hit. Again, no such report was made in Prescott newspapers at the time. And Prescott newspapers did not have the time to investigate such claims during the days shortly after the Great Fire. They were focused on getting back into the game.

A child at the time of the fire, and living with her parents on North Granite Street, Little Belle and her family vacated their house. She watched the fire from the plaza, as did many. When the Campbells returned to their home, it was gone. They slept near Granite Creek the next night, which she said was dry. The family rebuilt on North Marina Street.

There also was a report of a man who had been hit by shotgun fire in front of Sam Hill's, but no details were given.

GRANITE STREET IS ATTACKED BY FLAMES
BEFORE MONTEZUMA STREET

The firefighting moved to Granite Street and its infamous red-light district. Now there was apprehension that the fire would devour the whole town. The 100 block sections of Montezuma and Granite Streets were in jeopardy. Word was sent to Hotel Burke to evacuate its guests—the fire was coming its way.

By now, most of the firefighting equipment owned by the four fire companies—the Dudes, the Toughs, the OKs and the Hook and Ladder—was pulled onto the plaza. The firefighters' concentration switched to dynamiting and rescuing whatever items they could save from the businesses in the fire's path.

Word traveled by telephone and telegraph about the catastrophe blooming in Prescott and reached outlying areas. Some Jerome residents hitched their wagons and began heading south. Many Phoenicians went to the railroad ticketing offices and booked rides to the mountain town to the north.

The first establishment hit after the Grandview House dynamiting debacle was the Union Saloon and Lodging House, with its wooden cribs forming a right angle on the southeast corner of Goodwin and Granite Streets. Although a popular watering hole, the Union was best known for being a highly frequented stop along Prescott's red-light district. It was a brothel with a saloon attached to it in the middle.

Bill Fitzgerald recalled the experience of Dago Martin, who was hustling about in the cellar of the Union Saloon, hoping to save some of the cases of booze stored down there. It was decided that the Union would be purposely brought down in hopes of checking the flames. Unaware of Martin's presence in the Union basement, the firefighters hurled a cache of dynamite into the middle of the saloon. Suddenly, the building above him disappeared, and he found himself staring up into a night sky brightened by the flames. Martin was nearly deaf for more than two weeks, but he thought it was a miracle that he lived through the experience.

The plaza-facing section of Montezuma Street (today's Whiskey Row) was still untouched at this point. However, the most combustible business in Prescott sat behind the Union Saloon and the red-light district side of Granite Street. It was Sam Hill's Hardware. It contained what was probably the largest and most varied inventory of supplies in Prescott, including ammunition, assorted petroleum products and even mining powder. "Everybody swears by Sam Hill's" was a popular local saying.

The dropping of the Union Saloon did not keep the flames from traveling farther north. Again, dynamite probably worsened the situation by throwing embers into the brisk wind. The fire intensified. A domino effect was now

Two ladies of the night posing in front of the remnants of the Union Saloon on the northeast corner of Granite and Goodwin Streets. *From Sharlot Hall Museum.*

The Granite Street portion of Block 13 was completely wiped out. This image looks north from Goodwin Street. *From Sharlot Hall Museum.*

in motion. Granite Street houses were igniting one by one—most of them bordellos. There was still hope of preventing Sam Hill's from igniting, but reality was setting in as well. Montezuma Street, north of Goodwin Street, most likely would light up soon.

After failing to extinguish the flames inside the OK Lodging House, Bert Lee had run to Sam Hill's to help pull its massive volume of goods to the plaza. He was in the process of rescuing some rifles when a nearby dynamite blast (probably from the Union Saloon) loosened part of the ceiling and just missed crashing down on him. Little inventory was saved from Sam Hill's.

When Lee reached the plaza with an armful of rifles, he saw looters fleeing east toward Union Street and disappearing to some hiding place. Unfortunately, several looters selfishly took advantage of the chaos and confusion and stole property that had been deposited on the plaza. Lee concluded that since there were no guards present, his services might be more useful elsewhere. No use risking his life "to save stuff for thieves," he told Pat Savage. Seeing that the fire was now moving north toward

Gurley Street, Lee hurried to his workplace, the OK Grocery Store on the northwest corner of that street and Granite Street. It was in danger of being looted as well.

When the flames attacked Sam Hill's Hardware from behind, residents may have had a passing thought about the Fourth of July their town chose not to publicly celebrate that year. What occurred was far more spectacular than any fireworks any of them had seen or heard in their lifetimes—and far more terrifying.

The intensity of the heat growing and expanding up Granite Street and Whiskey Row Alley was too much for the products remaining in Sam Hill's Hardware. Ammunition of all sorts, kegs of gunpowder, barrels of mining powder and petroleum products and a host of other combustible items exploded, causing sights and sounds overwhelming to the eye and ear.

The fire escalated into an inferno. This is where a seemingly unstoppable momentum took over. The fire began to develop its own weather and wind pattern—one that could no longer be predicted. So intense was the heat that the hose the Toughs and Dudes had thrown down on Montezuma Street near the start of the fire melted. The people of Prescott now began to think that this fire was no ordinary fire but one that might prove epic.

The remains of Sam Hill's Hardware can be seen to the left. Behind it on Granite Street, Prescott's Chinatown is remarkably and totally intact. *From Sharlot Hall Museum.*

Hose carts, such as the one seen here, were left in the street and damaged by the intensity of heat from the Great Fire. *From Sharlot Hall Museum.*

Dynamiting became a pattern—most of it led by Johnny Robinson, a fireman who had some experience using dynamite for mining purposes, and Tommy Johns, a deputy sheriff. They sent an expressman, Mike Fagan, to fetch mining powder from wherever he could find it. He repeatedly made trips back and forth to the fire.

Seeing that the fire was surely going to take Montezuma Street, the Western Union office, set up in Hotel Burke, moved to Goldwater's on Cortez Street.

Some people later recalled that most able-bodied Prescottonians—hundreds according to more than one report—were assisting the firemen and business owners in some way. Gail Gardner was happy to say that even lawyers were running into stores, restaurants and saloons to help haul merchandise to safety. A horde of women and children gawked from the plaza.

Charles Ryland, a sign painter, commandeered a butcher's horse and hitched it to his own cart. He then encouraged people to load it up with their goods. At some point, Ryland was getting so many requests to use his cart that he threw the horse's reins into the air. Anyone lucky enough to grab them had his blessing.

This extraordinary image shows Montezuma Street in flames. Many people watched from the plaza as Whiskey Row burned. *From Sharlot Hall Museum.*

It was said that some business owners refused to help fight the fire and focused on saving only their own businesses. One was Morris Goldwater—the late Senator Barry Goldwater's uncle—who admitted that he concentrated on saving his store. One manager of an unnamed mercantile store was chastised for his selfishness after refusing to provide supplies to help fight the fire. After being asked, he said his business seemed safe from the fire, and he wanted to keep his items to sell later.

The swirling winds tossed popping embers in every direction with each ensuing dynamite blast. This, coupled with the intensifying heat, was leading to an out-of-control situation.

THE SIGHT AND SOUNDS DURING THE GREAT FIRE

The countryside all around Prescott was illuminated. Roosters crowed because they thought morning had come. One witness said he could read a newspaper from Mount Vernon Street.

Imagine being a five-year-old while this unimaginable event was happening. Daniel Seaman was just that. He recalled "being awakened in the night by a tumultuous confusion to witness flame and smoke towering high in the sky. A weird unearthly light illuminated the countryside with brilliance." When the fire, roaring like a massive smelter, hit one of its several acmes, "the scene was beyond all power of description," said Seaman. When the blaze hit un-rescued barrels of whiskey, brilliant blue flames shot into the sky.

The sounds of the conflagration matched its awful beauty. There were the shrieks of frightened horses being released from stables and herded toward Miller Valley. A few of these horses were driven to the plaza. There was the crackling roar of the fire itself, metal roofs groaning from the extreme heat and men shouting. "One's ears were assailed by warning shouts to 'get outa thar, they're going to blow up the buildin','" Harry Brisley said.

Explosions created pandemonium when flames met powders, bullet and shotgun cartridges, gasoline and oil. Time after time, the hills surrounding Prescott echoed with the boom of dynamite as firefighters futilely attempted to stay ahead of the fire. Mercy Hospital, more than a half mile northwest at 220 Grove Avenue, where Prescott College is located today, lost much of its ceiling plaster from the reverberations of dynamite detonations.

Kathryne Major, a young girl who would years later become Bill Fitzgerald's wife, remembered seeing from her childhood home in Groom Creek—six miles southeast from Prescott and almost one thousand feet higher in elevation—a reddened sky to the north and west. She realized even as a little girl that Prescott was afire.

BLOCK 13 CONTINUES TO BE ATTACKED BY MAMMOTH FLAMES

When the ingenious residents of Prescott's Chinatown on South Granite Street and the east bank of Granite Creek saw the fire moving their way, they grabbed quilts and cushions, placed them on the roofs of their houses and businesses and the joss house (a sacred place because it was their church and where their men's clubs met) and soaked them with water they had hauled and stored from the creek. They had been watching flying embers land on rooftops and lighting up buildings.

Several images taken after the Great Fire reveal that the flames circumvented the Chinese quarters. The only damage reported in Chinatown was that a Qing Dynasty dragon flag atop the joss house burned up.

But there were many close calls. One occurred near Granite Creek, where a powder house—a shed holding one thousand pounds of blasting powder—was located. A freelancer, known as Tommy, was spotted by two firemen crawling "crab-fashion" from underneath it. When asked, "What the hell are you doing?" Tommy, not knowing what was in the shed, said that he had placed five sticks of dynamite underneath it and lit the fuse with the idea of preventing the flames from reaching Prescott's west side. The two firemen dived underneath and pulled the fuse in the nick of time, saving the shack, Chinatown and west Prescott.

The fire was encroaching on the famous Montezuma Street saloons, the first of which was Cob Web Hall. Its owner, Judge "J.J." Hawkins, called out to all within earshot to "come and get it." The saloon's well-stocked shelves quickly emptied before the establishment was blown up. Soon after, Hawkins realized he had left his coat, carrying much money, on the back of a chair.

Faro layouts, roulette tables, cash drawers and registers, money from gaming tables, safes, varieties of merchandise, furniture, personal belongings and, of course, barrels and bottles of whiskey and kegs of beer were pulled out of Cob Web Hall, the Cabinet, the Palace and other Whiskey Row saloons.

Many tried to save coveted items. According to firefighter Worth Rybon of the OK Company, that was cigars for one man. Running with an armload of his favorite smoking pleasure, the man was a little too close to the action when another cache of dynamite exploded. A two-by-four rocketed his way and struck him square in the seat of his pants. The victim and cigars both went flying.

The Cabinet Saloon's famous cabinet of ore specimens, however, could not be saved. Cabinet owners Belcher and Smith had turned down many offers and gobs of money in the past to keep it in their saloon.

An amusing story occurred during the dynamiting of the Montezuma Street saloons. It involved the Cabinet Saloon's colorful co-proprietor Barney Smith. The aforementioned miner and fireman Johnny Robinson, tasked to carry out some of the dynamiting, entered the Cabinet carrying a twenty-five-pound box of miner's powder on his shoulder. Smith, still inside the Cabinet saving what he could, asked Robinson what he was planning to do. Robinson replied, "Blow up your place."

The flabbergasted Smith cried out, "Hell!" and asked where he planned to place the powder.

Robinson answered, "In the ice chest."

Smith's unexpected response was, "That's be dam' bad for the ice chest."

At one point, an intoxicated man wrestled a rifle from a guard stationed to deter looting. After firemen Pat Farley and Robinson subdued the belligerent fellow, it was discovered that he had stolen dynamite and booze.

So great was the heat from the fire that from time to time items removed from buildings would spontaneously burst into flames. Fred Brecht, the popular blacksmith and mayor pro tem, and Jake Weber, a nozzleman with a fire company, removed a sideboard to the streets and sprinted back into the building for more items. When they returned, they found the sideboard in ashes.

All manner of animals and pets were brought to the plaza. Cats did not fare so well. Prescott must have been quite the stray cat town. One of the more unforgettable observations was that hundreds of cats were found burned to death just by being near the fire's swath.

Now the fire was heading toward the Palace Saloon. Twenty-five years after the fire, firefighter Bob Morrison recalled that a group of men carried the piano from that saloon onto the plaza. The pianist Ed Wilson, probably one of that group, was followed by a singer described as a "painted lady." When the piano was situated properly, Wilson sat down and started hammering out a popular song of that day, the appropriately inappropriate "There'll Be a

Dynamite blasts sent debris out onto the streets. *From Sharlot Hall Museum.*

Hot Time in the Old Town Tonight," while the saloon girl sang heartily and the fire burned across the street.

Evidence indicates that this is more than just a good story. The testimony of William Greenwood, an eyewitness to the fire, an employee of Sam Hill's Hardware and formerly one of Theodore Roosevelt's Rough Riders confirmed, "Even a piano was moved to the new location, and soon someone was playing 'There'll Be a Hot Time in the Old Town Tonight.'"

The song caught on and was sung several times. At one point, people from as far away as Granite Street were heard singing along after the roar of the fire moved east, and soon seemingly half the town joined in. One report claimed that when Wilson reached the chorus during one of his renditions, another dynamite explosion from a nearby building caused an iron bar to be hurled in his direction. Luckily, it flew directly over his head and smashed into a hose cart.

Perhaps the most famous story regarding the Great Fire is that of Palace patrons carrying its bar across the street to the plaza. For many years, local historians and Palace proprietors and enthusiasts sparred over whether this legend was true. Indeed, no contemporaneous reports of that happening exist. However, a little detective work and some recently discovered research material end that dispute.

10

THE LEGEND OF THE PALACE BAR

rior to the release of The History Press's *Prescott's Original Whiskey Row* in November 2015, there had been some debate (sometimes heated) between local historians and Whiskey Row business owners and regulars as to whether what is perhaps Prescott's most famous and cherished legend is true. That is, the story of Palace patrons pulling the saloon's bar—the same bar sitting in the Palace today—out to the plaza while the inferno was racing north up Montezuma Street. Several sincere and legitimate local historians concluded that it is nothing more than fiction.

And for good reason. It has been thought by some that such an incident would surely have been reported around the time that it happened if it did indeed happen. What is probably true is that it did not seem newsworthy at the time. Thousands and thousands of items were pulled out to the plaza during the Great Fire. Why report just this one? The Palace's bar was no more important than any other rescued article at that time, and surely it was not the only bar pulled out. And no one could have predicted that the Palace Restaurant and Saloon would become what it has become today—that the incident would matter more than one hundred years later.

The story has been passed down through oral history. This, too, has rendered doubt in some minds because there is no actual documentation to prove its veracity. As mentioned in the previous chapter, recent evidence leaves no room for doubt. Therefore, we'll delve into a fuller history of the celebrated Palace bar.

The front and back walls of the Palace Saloon resisted the conflagration's intense heat and stood firm. *From Sharlot Hall Museum.*

Around six o'clock on Friday evening, November 5, 1897, a "lurid glare" was seen from one of the windows of the Palace Saloon. Like so many times before along Whiskey Row, shouts of "fire!" were heard. This fire would test the Palace's brick, stone and iron.

The source of the 1897 fire was a broken pipe above the steak fryer in the kitchen. The fire gained impetus, and flames burst through the popular saloon's front windows, shattering glass and electric light rondures. The firemen arrived with a swiftness that was compared to fire departments in larger cities. They quickly extinguished the flames.

The interior of the Palace was badly damaged, but the brick, stone and iron did the job they were expected to do and contained the fire. If the Palace had not been fashioned from these materials, a repeat of the 1883 Whiskey Row fire, when flames spread quickly to neighboring buildings, would have ensued.

The wooden portions in the saloon area burned to a crisp, as the *Miner* informed, "The front end of one of the most handsomely finished and best-appointed saloons in Arizona presented a charred mass of ruins while the water stood six inches on the floor."

Of great significance, the solid walnut bar, fitted after the Goodwin Street Palace Saloon was moved to Montezuma Street in 1884, was destroyed. It would have to be replaced. Total damages were estimated at $5,000. Insurance arrived promptly, and Bob Brow began rebuilding.

Requiring only fifty-three days to reconstruct, the Palace reopened on December 28. It was a festive event. A brass band welcomed a throng that agreed that the new Palace was a work of art: "Everything about the place betokens both elegance and taste," read the *Miner*.

Some notable changes were made. One, the Palace's restaurant and dining section were moved to the rear, making it separate from the saloon. A side entrance to the dining area was created so that, according to the *Miner*, "ladies who objected to entering a saloon, may be properly served."

Second, a new bar was installed, which most likely came by train from a Brunswick, Balke and Collender store in San Francisco. The *Miner*'s description of the bar is historically significant because it offers proof that it was the same bar that people were leaning on, and enjoying a drink from, on July 14, 1900. It stated, "The new bar is one of the handsomest in the south-west. It is made of cherry and is massive in proportions and finished in the most elaborate and artistic style."

The Palace Restaurant and Saloon's famous bar can be seen in this image, circa 1898. *From Sharlot Hall Museum.*

The celebrated bar in the Palace Restaurant and Saloon today was pulled out to the plaza during the Great Fire of 1900. *From Norman Fisk.*

This report and photographic evidence prove that it was the same Palace bar being used when the Great Fire of 1900 struck Whiskey Row; it is plainly seen in the only known pre–Great Fire image of the Palace. Additionally, a section of it is visible in one of the best-known photographs taken shortly after the fire, that of "Brow's Palace and not ashamed of it" photograph taken on the plaza in Brow's temporary makeshift saloon (see chapter 13).

The legend about this now-famous piece of furniture being saved during the Great Fire has proven true. Ideas as to how this occurred vary. Some say men hooked horses to it and dragged the bar out. Oxen have been credited for doing the same, as have men. However, even as extraordinary as it has proven to be, it was not even mentioned in reports of the many anniversaries and reunions that occurred over the years. It became a legend through spoken word and then a proven fact through intensive and careful research.

The celebrated bar is still there today and is photographed by visitors on a daily basis.

11

THE GREAT FIRE REACHES GURLEY STREET

The Palace Saloon of 1884 up to the Great Fire, as mentioned, was constructed of brick, stone and iron and was bypassed for dynamiting. Perhaps the firefighters had learned a lesson from the Grandview House fiasco. Perhaps they hoped the solid materials would stop the fire. However, the Palace quickly became another victim of its path. Portions of its brick walls stood firm, but most of it crumbled to the ground under the intense heat.

Now the fire, like a living thing, had its sights on the southwest corner of Montezuma and Gurley Streets, where the magnificent Hotel Burke stood. One of Harry Brisley's pharmacies was located in Hotel Burke. He recalled a certain madam of a good-sized rooming house whose lack of inhibition and self-consciousness proved advantageous. While helping to remove items from Brisley's store as the fire moved toward the Burke, the madam would lift the front of her skirt and allow store clerks to load it up with merchandise. She would then run out to the plaza, drop to her knees and unload the cargo, then rush back for more. Some men found this unforgettable.

When all efforts at dynamiting failed to stop the fire on Montezuma Street, and as the establishments burned one by one, hope turned to Hotel Burke. Its proprietors had for years flaunted it as the "only absolutely fireproof Hotel in Prescott."

Vice mayor, blacksmith and volunteer firefighter Fred Brecht told those at a gathering during the twenty-fifth anniversary of Prescott's most catastrophic event that by the time the fire reached Hotel Burke, the fire was burning and snarling like a smelter.

This stack of items across from the destroyed Palace Saloon may include its bar. *From Sharlot Hall Museum.*

Hotel Burke stood no chance. So incredibly powerful was this inferno that, by this time about midnight, as the first defiant flames licked the three-story structure, it was engulfed and went down within a span of five to ten minutes. Its wooden porches on each of the three levels were the first to go.

Later, it was written in the *Prospect*, a publication that was started in Prescott near the time of the Great Fire, "When the thousands of people who stood helpless on that memorable night saw the hungry flames devour the old Hotel Burke, there were many a sad heart among the throng, for they saw being swept away one of the finest buildings in the city, and well knew all of the hard work of patient labor and planning it had taken Messrs. Burke & Hickey."

By 12:30 a.m., the west side across from the plaza, Block 13—from Goodwin to Montezuma to Gurley Streets—was gone. This included the "badlands," the local nickname for the red-light district. The "fiery forks," which had grown to a fiery mass, mocked all efforts to tame them. It was reported that at this point more than a dozen buildings had been blown up.

A report came out of Jerome at 1:30 a.m., stating, "With no opposition the fire spread through the business district in a twinkling and at this hour, 1:30 o'clock, and is threatening a large portion of the town, with no possibility of checking it."

This stunning image taken from Gurley Street, most likely from the west, shows that the Hotel Burke was totally overwhelmed by the inferno. *From Sharlot Hall Museum.*

Portions of the walls of the Palace Saloon and Hotel Burke survived, but the rest were no match for the inferno. *From Sharlot Hall Museum.*

The "badlands" of Block 13 were devoured by the conflagration. *From Sharlot Hall Museum.*

The embers continued to eject northward across Gurley Street. The Kelly and Stephens Store, on the northwest corner of that street and Montezuma, went up like paper because it was, in part, a stationery store. Of course, by now, firefighters had to deal with more than flying embers. The heat from the massive flames had grown to such intensity that anything made of wood within one hundred feet was in danger of spontaneously igniting.

The focus of fighting the fire now shifted to the block encompassed by Gurley to the south, Granite to the west, Willis to the north and Montezuma to the east. Since the fire seemed to be heading directly north, the block east of Montezuma Street appeared safe. Unfortunately, that proved false. In the alley behind the Brinkmeyer Hotel—the second building east of Montezuma and facing the plaza on Gurley Street—stood a high barn used as a storage warehouse. From nothing more than the conflagration's intensity of heat, the barn exploded into flames. Like Montezuma Street, the fire attacked Gurley Street from behind.

This development jeopardized not only north but also east Prescott. A meat market attached to the west wall of the brick Brinkmeyer Hotel was blown up in hopes of saving the hotel. That effort failed like all others before it.

Just like Montezuma Street above Goodwin Street, the blaze initially attacked the plaza-facing section of Gurley Street from behind. *From Sharlot Hall Museum.*

Jake Marks's liquor dispensary, in the center of the plaza-facing Gurley Street buildings, was now at risk. Sometime before the fire turned the corner eastward on Gurley, someone asked Marks if he, like other Whiskey Row businessmen, wanted to move his products onto the plaza. Marks's reply was honest and classic: "No. We'd just start drinking and never get this fire out." This was not helpful. Marks's liquors were highly flammable. The fire hit his store and once again gained strength.

The Bank of Arizona on the northeast corner of Gurley and Cortez Streets was undergoing major improvements at the time. For that purpose, a large pile of lumber sat nearby. It was now in danger of catching fire and increasing the conflagration's already uncontrollable strength. Harry Brisley, whose second pharmacy was across the street on the northwest corner of Gurley and Cortez Streets, noticed "a ten-gallon tank of highly charged soda water" that had been pulled out of a store and onto the street. He opened the valve and pointed a twenty-five-foot stream at the lumber. The carbonated water successfully squelched the flames.

Brisley's Old Corner Drug Store—with a famous advertisement that read, "Cross the street to Brisley's Drug Store. You'll never live to regret it"—would need more than soda water to save it. It was quickly targeted for dynamiting with the aim of keeping the fire from crossing to the east side

Gurley Street businesses were able to pull out more inventory than those of other streets. *From Sharlot Hall Museum.*

Harry Brisley's Old Corner Drug Store was dynamited to prevent the fire from crossing to the east side of Cortez Street. *From Sharlot Hall Museum.*

The Gurley Street portion facing the plaza was destroyed before the fire traveled north onto Cortez Street. *From Sharlot Hall Museum.*

of Cortez Street and igniting east Prescott. It worked, but with the winds still blowing northward, the fire made a left turn and began to attack the buildings on the west side of Cortez Street.

But there was still the danger of flying embers.

THE BOY HEROES OF EAST PRESCOTT

Perhaps the most endearing episode during the Great Fire is that of two young boys who became the heroes of east Prescott. While flames were gobbling the buildings facing the plaza on Gurley Street, the fire had been racing eastwardly toward Cortez Street. The west side of Cortez was often considered an extension of Whiskey Row; it was the home of several saloons. The east side of Cortez, however, had been known as "Office Row" for probably as long as that row named after whiskey. But in the past, Prescottonians were prouder of Office Row than Whiskey Row.

If the fire continued to behave the same as it had for the previous nearly three hours, Office Row looked to be next on its list of victims.

At the junction of Gurley and Cortez Streets, a hundred-man bucket brigade formed. It is likely that someone finally discovered the water previously released into the mains by city water engineer John Love. On the northeast corner stood the Bellevue House, where two unidentified boys climbed the roof. Because soaring embers were creating so much havoc, the boys were instructed by the bucket brigade men to douse any embers landing on Office Row roofs with the buckets of water they hoisted up to them. If a bucket was not available, the nimble boys kicked the embers to the street. They energetically did this for at least an hour.

Some people believed the boys' efforts saved as much as ten blocks of east Prescott, although that is probably an exaggeration. Nonetheless, the fire did not cross Cortez Street, and the hero boys played a big part in preventing that from happening. Both received minor burns.

12

THE FIREFIGHT ON WEST CORTEZ STREET AND SUCCESS AT LAST

At one point, John Gardner, owner of a popular mercantile store on the east side of Cortez Street and the father of Prescott's legendary cowboy poet Gail Gardner, believed it was possible that the entire town of Prescott might burn to the ground. Consequently, he retrieved his delivery wagon, loaded up the store's cash register and ledgers and parked the wagon in front of his house. If it looked like all of Prescott was going to be reduced to ashes, he was ready to ride out of town with his family and money.

The only serious injury caused by the fire was to Ed Harrold. In chapter 7, it is mentioned that Harrold has been incorrectly labeled by some Prescott historians as the man who jabbed the miner's candlestick holder into a wall of an OK Lodging House room, leaving the candle burning only to have it fall on a bed. Harrold was a former Prescott resident but had moved to Flagstaff, where he lived for five years. Ironically, he had returned to Prescott for the first time on the very night of the Great Fire and would forever be linked with it.

Harrold rented a room at the Bellevue Hotel on the northeast corner of Cortez and Gurley Streets. When he saw the fire racing east on Gurley Street, he decided to pitch in to help save the hotel. Harrold was engaged with "pulling down the porch" when a fragment from an unknown source fell from above and struck him squarely on the head, rendering him unconscious. He was sent to Mercy Hospital.

The fire took a northerly turn here from Gurley to Cortez Street. *From Sharlot Hall Museum.*

Although the east side of Cortez was not afire, the flames on the west side of that street maintained their momentum and headed north toward Willis Street. If it crossed Willis, the train depot at the junction on Sheldon Street would be in its path. The train was considered perhaps the most critical tool for Prescott's prosperity. It was feared that the train cars parked at the depot were in trouble. They would have to be moved if the flames threatened them. But they were needed. The post office also was in jeopardy of being taken by the flames, and the mail needed to be moved to a safe location. The train cars would offer a secure place. All of Prescott's mail and many other important documents belonging to the city and its businesses were moved into the cars.

The fire never reached the depot. One more building at the corner of Cortez and Willis was dynamited. And suddenly it was over.

Chief of Police Steve Prince surveys the Great Fire's swath of destruction. *From Sharlot Hall Museum.*

REST AT LAST

Harry Brisley noted, "It was reported that Brow, Belcher and Smith of the Palace [and Cabinet] had tapped kegs of cold beer nearby the courthouse and was free to all comers. Never had been heard more welcome news after five hours of continuous toil." Much to their disappointment, the two young hero boys of Cortez Street were told they were not invited to this party but that they should go on home and rest. They also were told they had most likely saved much of east Prescott. Happy to hear this but disheartened that their heroics had not proved a rite of passage, the two soot-covered heroes sauntered home.

The burned-out area of Prescott was in near total darkness now because electric lights, poles and wires were destroyed. Candles and lanterns were in short supply. Most of the telephones were out of order. But now, the people could take a break for the first time in five hours. They waited for the daylight that would reveal the panoramic aftermath of this devastating and epic event. The Great Fire had ripped the guts right out of their town.

Even as the fire burned, and after it ended, there was never the thought of abandoning this place they called "Preskitt." Over and over it has been said that the people of Prescott bore the appalling outcome of the fire in a philosophical, almost joyful manner. They viewed it as the eve of rebirth for Prescott and Whiskey Row. They saw it as an opportunity.

13

NO TIME FOR GLOOMINESS—THE REBUILD BEGINS

As the sun rose on Sunday, July 15, Prescottonians, through bloodshot eyes, took in the sight of devastation. It was terrible to behold. Shells of buildings stood like specters. Wood and tin filled the streets—thrown there by dynamite blasts.

The first Prescott newspaper to put out a publication after the fire was the town's gossip rag, the *Howler*. For reasons unknown, Bob Brow of the Palace bought as many copies as he could. Perhaps he realized that particular issue's historical significance.

The *Miner*, in which the editor understatedly acknowledged that it "had received a blow," was able to put out a paper on July 19, using a press donated by the *Arizona Republican*. That edition was distributed for free, and it joked, "Prescott never does anything by halves, and our fire was the biggest any town in the territory ever had. We are proud to lead." In that same edition, Prescott's optimism shone brightly to the point of being blinding, predicting, "Wait until you see the new Prescott and you will say the fire brought forth the true emerging of our energetic mountain people."

The *Courier* lost everything but thirty cases of type, so it was scrounging for replacements. Before the fire, it bragged that it was "one of the largest 4-page [apparently referring to the size of the pages] papers on earth." By the time September arrived, the paper company was still waiting for a power press to arrive that would enable a larger paper to be printed again.

The *Courier* people were in dire straits all the way around. With headquarters destroyed, its owner put forth a plea in a most polite and

Prescott before the Great Fire of 1900. *From Nancy Burgess.*

Prescott shortly after the Great Fire of 1900. *From Nancy Burgess.*

humble manner. The newspaper was $4,000 in debt, which was mostly due to unpaid subscriptions. That sum of money had a purchasing power equivalent today of a whopping $110,000. The owner, Edward Rogers, wrote, "Now is the accepted time for people to come forward and settle up, for this paper needs the money, and those who owe have been having the free use of our paper for a long time."

Rogers continued, "The proprietor of this paper is over 40 years old, has always kept his debts paid up under all sorts of circumstances; and he is a man of very ordinary ability, knows that other men can do the same." Finally, he wrote, "We are not working any sympathy racket, but simply call for what we have honestly earned now that we need it badly and will receive it thankfully." The *Courier* moved to Goose Flats, where the Mile High Middle School football field is currently located. The building was described as "a lopsided stable."

The *Miner* was only able to save some of its books and ledgers. Lost was a Mergenthaler linotype that had been purchased only three months before the fire.

In spite of the vaunted Prescott optimism, an expected momentary feeling of gloom pervaded the town that was now in ashes. To add to the prevailing despair, the wind escalated, causing clouds of blinding smoke and dust to envelop the town. Every now and then the winds would spark, sending a threatening ember into the air toward the unburned part of town, keeping everyone on edge.

Three and a half blocks were destroyed—truly the guts of Prescott. Some reports claim that two-thirds of the town was consumed by the flames. Gone were all of its saloons: The Palace, Cabinet, Cobweb, Kearney's, Companos, Union, Headquarters, Sazerac, Comet and Cellar, to name a few. More than seventy businesses were listed as destroyed. The estimated total loss of $1,500,000 would be by today's standard approximately $45,000,000.

The approximate monetary losses per business came in quickly. The Bashford-Burmeister Company of Gurley Street was hit hardest by far, suffering a shocking $250,000 loss. Next was Sam Hill's Hardware, losing $80,000. Hotel Burke, with a $66,000 loss, was third. Jake Marks lost $25,000, and much of that sum came from his liquors being swallowed by the flames. Amazingly, the Palace and Cabinet saloons—whose histories would soon be enhanced to an even greater level—were low on the list, both losing $10,000 worth of property. Fifteen saloons lost between $1,000 and $3,000 each.

Gusts of winds occasionally blew smoke and embers into the air for days after the Great Fire. *From Sharlot Hall Museum.*

The *Arizona Republican* told its readers that "this is enough to discourage any other Arizona town, but Prescott cannot afford to be discouraged." Yes, not Prescott.

A goal of upgrading inevitably follows a disaster. This would prove an understatement for Prescott. Its indomitable spirit was more intact than ever. There was no time to waste for these resilient frontier people. Gloom quickly turned into determination and hope. Indeed, it was Prescott's historic pivotal point.

Residents began to get excited about a "New Prescott." Already, they were clearing away debris to make way for it. One victim noted that "while the ruins were smoking and some of them yet blazing," citizens were preparing to temporarily relocate. Another victim wrote to his brother, "We got through fighting the fire about 4 or 4:30 and by 8 A.M., we were hauling lumber [to the plaza] to build again. No one seems discouraged."

The *Prospect*, now the best-written newspaper in Prescott, would remember it this way:

> *With all the frightful destruction of that night we, at this time, fail to remember having seen but very few sad faces. True, a great many had*

grievances but hardly time to air them. When daylight came never was there such a scene as the one witnessed on the plaza. Men, women and children with blood-shot eyes could be seen on every side, but their demeanor was as cheerful as if they were at a picnic. Everything from a box of sardines to a five hundred dollar piano was there, but to, but to the everlasting benefit of Prescott many an old bed bug rookery was gone, and while it seemed hard on that morning we believe the majority will say amen.

As a precaution, a few men patrolled the scene of devastation looking for flare-ups. Cash drawers and registers, safes and money from the gambling tables rescued during the fire were taken to the sheriff's office, which became Prescott's financial center for several weeks. The need for this proved so great that a second financial center was set up in the courthouse.

Immediately, Prescott's board of supervisors and the sheriff's office got busy getting Prescott rolling again. The plaza, which had never functioned as anything other than a public-use space during its thirty-six years of existence, became the temporary business district. Forty-six lots on the perimeter of the plaza were divvied up, most of which were on Montezuma

While the ruins of Prescott were still smoldering, plans were being made for a new Prescott. *From Sharlot Hall Museum.*

and Gurley Streets. Some outsiders wanting to capitalize on Prescott's plight tried to steal some of these lots, but they were easily evicted.

The Gurley Street portion was labeled Enterprise Avenue, while the Montezuma Street side was called First Avenue. Business owners were given space equal to what they occupied before the fire. These lots were premium and highly desired. One owner of a fifty-six-foot fronting was offered an enticing $400 per square foot. He refused and set up shop for himself.

Thankfully, the fire did not touch the town's three lumberyards. An army of carpenters got busy and began putting up temporary quarters on the plaza. "Piles of new lumber and brick piled in front of the long rows of ruins tell plainer than words can what is to be done," read the *Miner*. Some businesses were up and running by Monday morning.

Whiskey continued to be served from a tent, within which were two beer barrels with a board across them and whiskey bottles atop, not too much unlike Prescott's first saloons in 1864.

Some later claimed that in the old Prescott stock interests were low, the mining industry was stagnant and there had been a general lethargy and standstill before the Great Fire. As mentioned, that is debatable. Whatever the case, Prescott was wide awake now.

Again, the *Prospect* described it best: "The spirit of aggressiveness exhibited by Prescott in her ordeal quickened the impulse of every man in the county; raising the cloud of indolence and discontent, causing all to admire each

The Gurley Street portion of "tent city" on the plaza was called Enterprise Avenue by locals. *From Sharlot Hall Museum.*

The Montezuma Street side of tent city was labeled First Avenue. *From Sharlot Hall Museum.*

other's vim and prowess, which in turn called the attention and admiration of the capitalist of the outside world, who in sticking his nose into our affairs found him a willing captive."

No one seemed to want to throw in the towel. Capitalist John Lawler, who had businesses on Cortez Street, said that although his former establishments were "surrounded by smoking embers and smouldering [*sic*] ruins, my faith in today is firmer and more loyal than ever before. Prescott, even in ashes, will rise. I am willing to stand by it and the last to desert it."

J.J. Hawkins was ready to rebuild his Cob Web Hall the day after the fire. His confidence was inspiring: "Prescott is destined to be the gem of the [Sierra Prieta Mountains] from an architectural and commercial standpoint. She has the mineral material in her backbone." Hawkins was the first to have his burned-out lot cleared off for rebuilding. In fact, he intended to not only rebuild the Cob Web on Montezuma Street with brick on his fifty-by-eighty-foot lot but also to build another fifty-by-seventy-five-foot business on Gurley Street.

Liquor wholesaler Jake Marks remarked, "It is useless to say I am going to throw up the sponge today." Then he went so far as to say, "This fire is a little setback, but the town will get there again, with both feet." Marks's statement typified the entrepreneurial frontier spirit of Prescott. No one was willing to let the dream of Prescott go.

Ben Belcher and Barney Smith of the Cabinet admitted that they had sustained a clean-cut knockout. Yet they, too, remained optimistic, saying

Prescott became the busiest place in Arizona after the Great Fire. *From Sharlot Hall Museum.*

that they were as "young and hopeful as ever to continue business at the old stand." At this point, they could not have imagined that they would soon be putting up a building as magnificent as Prescott had ever seen—one that still stands today as the heart and gem of Whiskey Row.

Michael Hickey and Dennis Burke of the Hotel Burke regretted that their hard work over the years to make their hotel the best in town, if not Arizona—one they believed was absolutely fireproof—had gone up in flames. However, "they gave it out flatfootedly today that they again take the 'bit in the mouth' and will erect a new hotel with a frontage of 100 feet on Montezuma and 150 feet on Gurley." The *Miner* went on to say, "The blow was a terrible one (for Burke and Hickey), and less brave hearts than theirs would have been crushed. Before the last embers of the old building had ceased to smoke, work had begun to clear the foundation for the new building."

Heartfelt letters poured in from all over the state. Perhaps the most important was one written by the acting territorial governor, Charles Akers, who telegraphed the *Miner* editor, John Martin, saying, "The Territory of Arizona extends its sympathy to the people of Prescott because of their deplorable loss by fire last night, and I feel that Phoenix, your sister city, if called upon, will not only extend sincere sympathy, but substantial aid."

Amazingly, Martin wired back that Prescott was not in need of any help. The general belief among Prescott citizens was that no outside aid would be needed at all. Of course, this was not true, but Prescott pride was robust. The *Howler*, true to form, teased that Phoenix did indeed help "us by sending up a car load of sightseers. They brought along their lunch." Within two days, the burned-down town was receiving an influx of out-of-town visitors. Curious Phoenix folks arriving by train wanted to get a glimpse of the desolation or help in any way they could, or perhaps both. People from Mayer also were riding the train into Prescott for the same reasons.

An encouraging letter came from A.L. Morrison, internal revenue collector for Arizona and New Mexico. It was intended to be a private communication to the editor of the *Miner*, but Martin believed everyone in Prescott should read it. Morrison was in Chicago when it was hit by its great fire in 1871. He reminded Martin that it was the first Chicago newspaper— "like a bright ray of hope"—that came out after the Windy City was in ashes "that the heavy clouds of despondency began to give way to the bright gleams of hope and courage." In another words, Morrison implied, Prescott needed to be led by its newspapers. And it would not be let down.

The issue of insurance quickly emerged. Because Prescott was perceived as a combustible town by insurers—they obviously could not have been more correct—rates were high and prohibitive for some business owners. Some proprietors were old school and carried no insurance at all. In the end, out of the estimated $1.5 million loss, only $250,000 would be reimbursed. Only eighteen businesses received 50 percent or more of their total losses from insurance. Insurance agents, however, were lauded for hurrying to tally the losses.

Also greatly appreciated among business owners was the fact that banks reduced interest rates for rebuilding loans. Loan companies chose to invest rather than run. They "thought it better to increase their loans on a renewal than to foreclose on a charred basement," stated the *Prospect* eighteen months after the Great Fire.

The Prescott Electric Company was highly praised and appreciated. In its efforts to restore lighting and telephone service, its workers were said to be acting with alacrity and tirelessness.

To get closer to the action, the Salvation Army established its headquarters on the east side of the plaza near Cortez Street underneath the sprawling branches of a cottonwood tree.

The only grocery store left in town was Joe Dougherty's OK Grocery Store, which was miraculously spared during the fire that somehow skirted his business—a fraction to the west of the fire's borders. Consequently, orders for food were sent to Jerome and Phoenix. Tommy Johns noted: "We sent a train and crew to Jerome with instructions to buy everything they could get, and we sent another scouting party to Congress for the same purpose. We contacted a representative of a coast firm and ordered a carload of canned goods to be shipped by express." Prescott was desperate for supplies—especially food.

Wholesalers flooded into town anxious to sell rebuilding materials and other items of necessity. Some were not welcomed because it was believed they were stealing business from local entrepreneurs. However, a little bit of humility on proud Prescott's part was necessary to get through this stage of its rebuild.

Ten new deputy sheriffs were sworn in to help keep the peace on the plaza, which would soon become a very busy and compact commerce borough.

The Western Union Office, moved during the fire to Goldwater's on the northeast corner of Goodwin and Cortez Streets, became a permanent fixture there. The post office was moved to the railroad depot because most mail was already stored in some of the boxcars.

Workers from the surrounding mining camps took time off and immediately flooded into town. Many came willing to pitch in, but they also sensed that they would be viewing something not only macabre but also historic. Because of this, those who had quickly erected their temporary quarters were doing a rip-roaring business.

Just two days after the fire, four saloons were open on the plaza and bringing in some coin. Planks of wood laid across whiskey and beer barrels still served as bars. New liquors were coming in from Phoenix and Congress and Jerome. Rebuilding was moving so fast that it was predicted that within a day there would be a dozen saloons on the plaza complete with musical and gaming opportunities.

That is why William Greenwood gave an alternate reason for the Prescottonians' legendary cheerfulness during this time: whiskey and beer flowed without restraint. A party atmosphere often filled the plaza. However, five-cent beers were no longer available. Because the demand for alcoholic drinks had risen, so did the prices. Nevertheless, saloons and restaurants—makeshift for sure—were collecting whatever they charged, and not in an inconsiderable quantity.

As an example of the good humor in Prescott after its worst disaster, clothing dealer Ed Block advertised, "Fire Sale! Not damaged by water nor by fire but slightly mussed and crushed." Block, however, was one of the few able to rescue every article from his store and was now selling his goods at manufacturers' cost.

As the tent and pine-shack city evolved, there was still a great concern that another fire could ignite because many of the buildings going up quickly on the plaza were flammable. The monsoon rains had not yet arrived. Every business up and running was supplied with a bucket of water to douse anything that might suddenly flare up. In fact, the winds were still strong as July moved toward August. Embers were still blowing here and there. A woman was arrested two days after the conflagration for making a fire in her yard.

Meals were going for thirty-five cents, but you could get extra by paying fifty cents. Most of the first restaurants on the plaza were run by the Chinese.

Charles Ryland, the sign painter who commandeered the butcher's horse when the flames grew out of control, was proud that his painting business was advertised in the *Howler* edition that was the first Prescott publication to appear after the Great Fire. Ryland later became a commercial photographer and then went into show business, traveling all around the world. In that capacity, he gained some fame.

Selling bricks suddenly became a booming business, and several new brickyards sprang up in town. The main one was owned by a Mr. Fitzsimmons in Miller Valley. By July 24, it was reported that stacks of bricks were forming in front of the ruins, and the first brick had been laid out by a contractor, F.G. Plummer, in the wall of a planned restaurant on Cortez Street.

Days after the fire, some Granite Street habitués, the "horizontal experts," attempted to set up shop on the plaza but were told they could not do their kind of business there. These prostitutes were instructed to move south below Goodwin Street where they would not be visible to the general public.

There was even talk at this time of preventing the rebuilding of the red-light district, which had been situated on the east side of Granite Street since the early 1870s, if not before. Some people hoped for classier buildings that would be used for loftier purposes. This effort, however, failed. John Sorg, owner of fifteen lots on that side of Granite and the northeast junction of Goodwin Street, rented his lots to former tenants who had operated saloons and brothels. Prescott's red-light district would instead be built in a more substantial style and, yes, even thrive as late as the 1940s.

As mentioned, none of Prescott's lumberyards were touched by the fire, but more timber was needed to build the temporary Prescott. Lumber was arriving by the carload at the train depot.

The few items saved from Sam Hill's proved extremely valuable. Kegs of nails were especially sought after. Canvas tents had been pulled out before the flames hit the hardware store and were now being used for temporary quarters on the plaza.

William Greenwood, an employee of Sam Hill's, set up a tent on the original burned-out site. From there he sold corrugated iron, iron stoves and, of course, nails. Sam Hill himself was back in town, back in charge and making crucial decisions.

Shortly after the Great Fire, the Hotel Burke's back wall, which had survived the fire, was razed by dynamite. By July 25, it was reported that a small army of boys was working hard cleaning and stacking brick for $1.50 per one thousand bricks for Dennis Burke and Michael Hickey. This took some time. According to Bill Fitzgerald—one of the boys cleaning and stacking brick that July—some of his so-called friends stole bricks from other boys' stacks hoping to more quickly hit their quota. This caused several fights among the youngsters. Most of the bricks cleaned and stacked by these boys are part of today's Hotel St. Michael.

The Hotel Burke proprietors hired young boys to clean and stack bricks that had fallen during the conflagration for $1.50 per one thousand bricks. *From Sharlot Hall Museum.*

Burke and Hickey also received a set of workhorses from a K. Barrett of Phoenix, formerly of San Francisco, where he operated a large wrecking company. It was reported that he felt "perfectly at home again." These strong animals were used to clear the ruins of the Burke Hotel to make way for the new building.

They announced that their new edifice would be 100 feet by 150 feet and four stories tall. This would cause some controversy because Prescott's city ordinance limited buildings to three stories. Much to Burke and Hickey's disappointment and anger, the city council enforced the ordinance. Local legend has it that out of revenge, the row of gargoyles seen today along Hotel St. Michael's third story were chosen to represent each of the city council members; therefore, the two owners picked the ugliest gargoyles they could buy.

Two newspapers were found inside the cornerstone of the old Hotel Burke: a July 11, 1890 *Courier* and a July 16, 1890 *Miner*. Miraculously, both were said to be as readable as the day they were published. How the papers got inside the cornerstone in the first place was not explained.

The plaza's bandstand, a site that had hosted many musical events since around 1880, became the temporary Palace Barbershop. On July 25, a bathhouse was reported to have been set up on the plaza next to the bandstand. "The bath house seems to be a small tent enclosing tubs resting on the ground," guessed the *Miner*.

At this time, Prescott was receiving some sprinkles, while the surrounding country was getting flooded with rain. "We are long on fire but short on rain," a report read.

By August 1, the *Courier* was able to say, "Prescott has the biggest building boom in its history." Temporary structures were being raised on the plaza while the foundations for the future permanent buildings were being laid. Ground for the new Hotel Burke foundation had been cleared. In the meantime, Burke and Hickey had moved their business into the Sherman House on North Montezuma Street and were preparing to open on August 1. However, they were in need of additional help. They telegraphed appropriate places in California asking "for female assistance and waitresses at good wages."

The residents also expected rain on August 1. To the disappointment of everyone, it did not materialize, although it did hit Skull Valley, twenty miles southwest of Prescott. With little water in town, several enterprising Mexicans transported water from down south to Prescott. Their business thrived for quite some time.

The plaza bandstand, seen here center, became a temporary barbershop. *From Sharlot Hall Museum.*

Astoundingly, smoke was still rising from the ruins in certain spots. Residents whose homes had not been touched by the Great Fire were asked to not light oil lamps for fear of igniting more fires. Whether or not this edict was enforced is not clear.

Ed Harrold, whose head had been injured during the night of the fire while trying to dismantle the porch of the Bellevue Hotel on the east side of Cortez Street, had recovered enough to be released from Mercy Hospital to a private house at Fort Whipple on August 3. For two weeks, he had remained partially conscious and mentally disoriented with rambling speech. His full recuperation was expected to be slow.

The reader might remember that a Qing Dynasty flag flown above Chinatown's joss house burned during the Great Fire. It was finally replaced on August 17. This riled a few local United States patriots. A group of them marched over to the Chinese quarters and demanded that an American flag be placed above the Chinese pennant. A heated parley followed. The Chinatown residents eventually agreed to the demand. Soon one man surfaced with an American flag—a full six inches long and four inches wide. The Chinese flag was hauled down, the little banner placed above it, and both were run to the top of the pole. In the end, everyone got a chuckle out of it.

Tents and shacks continued to multiply along the plaza. More than one eyewitness described the scene as taking on the appearance of far north gold mining camps like Camp Nome or Klondike and especially

Dawson City of the Yukon. One business owner claimed it took on such an appearance less than four days after the fire.

The north side of the plaza facing Gurley Street was already filled solid with shacks. The west side of the plaza facing Montezuma Street was close to being filled while the east side was half full. The whole plaza area was soon named Dawson City but was sometimes referred to as "Shantyville" or "Burg Forty-Nine."

Several "camp followers of disaster" had come into town bringing second-rate goods to sell at high prices when the Dawson City merchants' stock got low. Of course, while necessary in the short term, this was not appreciated. With a bit of forceful encouragement, they were soon chased out of town after their presence—and goods—were no longer required.

Robert Brow gathered lumber, tin and other building materials and placed them on the plaza about forty yards south of Palace's pre-fire location. He spread a white canvas tarpaulin over these materials and all items rescued when the flames were heading toward his saloon, including the magnificent bar that rests in the Palace today. Also present was the base of the back bar. The back bar itself and wooden icebox seen in a late 1890s image of the Palace's interior were either destroyed during the fire or replaced after it.

As tents and shacks went up on the plaza, it reminded some of far north mining camps, especially Dawson City of the Yukon. *From Sharlot Hall Museum.*

Dawson City on Montezuma Street. *From Sharlot Hall Museum.*

When his tin and wooden shack was completed, Brow posted a sign above the saloon doors that read, "BROW'S PALACE AND NOT ASHAMED OF IT." Through those doors a portion of the now famous Palace Restaurant and Saloon bar, still in use today, can clearly be seen. Brow also advertised on the front of his building that he still had a Dutch oven and sold Dexter Whiskey. He had another Dutch oven anchored on Montezuma Street, north of Gurley Street.

Cabinet Saloon proprietors Ben Belcher and Barney Smith relocated a few yards from Brow's makeshift Palace. Two tent-like constructions covered in white canvas eventually became "a commodious frame structure." Notably, this proximity to Brow's Palace enabled the three men, already close friends, to easily communicate with one another. This would prove historic.

When exactly the three businessmen made that happy decision to merge their businesses—the two most popular saloons on Whiskey Row prior to the Great Fire—into a single grand establishment is not known. More than one report claims that the idea germinated the day after the Great Fire when the ruins of their former buildings were still smoldering. That is not possible. In the middle of August, Belcher and Smith were making plans for their new Cabinet building and had not yet partnered with Brow.

A portion of the Palace bar, still in use today, can be seen through the doors of Bob Brow's temporary quarters on the plaza. *From Sharlot Hall Museum.*

Whenever it occurred, they decided to build a saloon that would be second to none in the West.

On August 10, the three entrepreneurs bought from Hugh McCrum of San Francisco Lot 19, where the Palace Saloon had operated since 1884; the joint-usage Lot 20 with its bathhouses, barbershops and dining areas; and Lot 21, where the Cabinet Saloon had thrived—in other words, addresses 118, 120 and 122 Montezuma Street.

The $7,000 paid for these lots was viewed as shockingly low. The *Courier* put it this way: "The lots would have been a bargain at $10,000. This is the cheapest piece of property sold in Prescott since the fire." Why McCrum sold these lots so inexpensively is not known. Perhaps he thought Prescott had been done in and wanted no part of it. Still, there was no mention of a partnership between these men. In fact, it was noted that "handsome buildings will be placed on all the lots," and Belcher and Smith would be erecting a separate building at a cost of $20,000.

Most likely, the decision to merge the Cabinet and Palace Saloons was made in late August or early September.

When the men did start building their grandly planned vision, Joe Petit was in charge. To finance the merger, Bob Brow, Ben Belcher and Barney Smith borrowed a certain amount of money—one report claimed it was $90,000, but that is probably high—from Joseph Mayer, founder of Mayer, Arizona. Mayer charged 1.5 percent interest.

Since this would be an amalgam of two former saloons, there was the issue of what to name their new establishment. At first, a decision was made to simply call it the Palace-Cabinet Saloon. Had the proprietors kept that name, the task of determining this saloon's birth year would have been much easier. In the past, historians have focused only on the name *Palace*, while not factoring in the fact that today's Palace Restaurant and Saloon is just as much the old Cabinet—origination year 1874—as it is the old Palace.

When the blueprints for the new building were being drawn up, a compromise was made. It would not be called the Palace or Cabinet, but the National Saloon, and was designated so on the back of the blueprints. Again, had it been dubbed so, its birth year would have been less difficult to establish—*Palace* would not have been fixated on by historians.

Probably when the three proprietors saw the idea behind those blueprints becoming a physical reality on Whiskey Row, "National Saloon" was crossed out and above it was written "Palace." After all, as the new Palace Saloon's first advertisement stated, "It's just what its name would imply."

Herman Voge set up his wholesale liquor business next to the Cabinet Saloon's temporary headquarters. If one wanted to keep drinking after imbibing at the Cabinet, it was easy enough to stop in and purchase a bottle or two from Voge's to take home.

A few inconsequential monsoon rains occurred in late July. Finally, a downpour fell on Prescott on August 17, flooding the countryside. Granite Creek became "riverlike." The gully washer forced one couple to fall into

Brow, Belcher and Smith initially agreed to name their new saloon the National Saloon but changed their minds along the way. *From Sharlot Hall Museum.*

the Union Saloon's cellar, which had filled with water. The man's suit was ruined, and he had to buy a new one.

On August 20, work commenced on the new Hotel Burke foundation. By mid-October, the basement was finished, and bricks had reached the top of the ground. Builders were racing to get this groundwork finished before the first frost hit. Most of the basement was composed of bricks saved after the Great Fire, and today some of them still have a charred appearance.

As the new Prescott was being raised, it was observed that most people were walking in the middle of its streets. Why? Concrete sidewalks were being laid in every direction. Progress was everywhere.

A desperately needed new waterworks was planned for Prescott. Ample water was a must for Prescott's survival and reconstruction. The subject of an essential water supply had been a vital but vexing one for more than three decades. Now there was no time to waste; a remedy was needed pronto. On September 29, it was reported that men and material had arrived at Del Rio Springs, north of Chino Valley and twenty-two miles from Prescott, and work would soon begin.

Virgil Earp, who had lived in Prescott with his wife, Allie, from 1877 through 1879, was back in town. In September, he had been on the Republican ticket for Yavapai County sheriff. However, Earp—whose left arm had been crippled after an assassination attempt while serving as the acting town marshal in Tombstone, Arizona—withdrew from the race. The *Courier* explained that he was "evidently a man with too much brains" to want the position.

On September 19 at eleven o'clock in the morning, fifty-eight-year-old Charles Smith died of a heart attack inside Bob Brow's Palace on the plaza. Smith had not been in Prescott long, arriving two months earlier from Kingman, where he had lived for eight years. He was said to have been "well connected." Fortune followed tragedy when, shortly after, a sporting man won $7,000 in a poker game in the makeshift Palace. This was a big score for that day—more than $200,000 in today's money.

Joseph Dougherty's OK Grocery Store had not been damaged during the fire, but he caught the rebuilding bug. Two weeks after the catastrophe, he was laying a foundation for a new building and making arrangements to expand into a general merchandise store. In fact, it was said that there would be a Dougherty Block in west Prescott, which at the time was any street west of Montezuma Street, Prescott's "Central Avenue."

Ironically, fire struck the old OK Store on October 1. Water was quickly turned on at the reservoir, and the gallant work of the volunteer fire department saved the store. Still, the fire destroyed other nearby properties that Dougherty owned, including his OK Restaurant.

By October, the *Prospect* predicted that "Montezuma street will have more up-to-date buildings within the next three months than any other town of like size in the southwest. The late fire wrought havoc with many, but, being imbued with the true western spirit of progress, the buildings now being erected in the wake of relentless flames are evidence that the people of Prescott have an abiding faith in the city of pines."

Concurrently with the rebuilding of Prescott, a gold rush was developing in the surrounding mountains. New discoveries of rich ledges were being reported, and a boom was expected. Locals felt like a new prosperity was hurrying their way. Many believed that the primary reason for rebuilding Prescott was because the mining industry demanded it.

On Tuesday, October 23, excitement filled the town when Governor Nathan Oakes Murphy paid a visit. According to the *Prospect*, "Never in the history of Arizona has there been a more patriotic gathering." Murphy's speech was called dispassionate, "avoiding personalities," which was refreshing to many. Of course, the political party opposing the governor interpreted his words much differently. His main topic was statehood, which was critical for many Prescottonians.

An odd report published in the *Courier* on October 27 stated that a "loud smell" pervaded the plaza. With no explanation as to why this was being done, the stench was said to have been "caused by the burning of $760 worth of lion and bear scalps."

Around that time, Quaker doctors visited Prescott, causing much curiosity among residents. Hundreds attended nightly meetings at the junction of Gurley and Cortez Streets. Quite a show was put on. Not only were there many healings, but the Quakers also brought dancers, comedians and a high-diving dog named Duke. As for the healings, it was believed by most that they were genuine and miraculous; even skeptics left the meetings as believers. Eventually, these Quakers were proven to be fakers when they were caught in a scandal in Phoenix.

Among the reported miracles was bringing hearing back to a previously deaf old soldier named Henry Pierce. After hearing the ticking of a watch in the distance, he was so grateful that he offered his next pension check to the Quakers. The response from the healing doctor was, "Friend, keep thy money; I need it not. I am glad to have benefitted thee; do not thank me, but thank thy Lord." Just as astounding, it was claimed that one J. McClean of Prescott had a 120-foot tapeworm delivered from his body.

As mentioned in a previous chapter, it has been incorrectly stated in several narratives of the Great Fire that the Cowboy Hall of Fame's George Ruffner was Yavapai County sheriff at the time and that he performed several great deeds during it. Perhaps he did, but the sheriff at that time was John Munds, a Democrat, and he was running for sheriff again in November 1900. Because Virgil Earp, a Republican, had withdrawn from the race, Munds was running unopposed until Ruffner, also a Democrat, decided to run as an independent—for which he was criticized. When the votes were tallied after Election Day, Munds remained in office.

Near the end of December, Jake Marks's liquor store was back in business at its old location on Gurley Street. Interestingly, the lot was owned by two prohibitionists: Ross and Sullivan.

THE PLAZA BEGINS TO CLEAR AND NEW PRESCOTT IS CLOSE TO BEING FINISHED

As 1900 rolled into 1901, reports of the rebuild were few and far between in the Prescott newspapers until the middle of that year. New Prescott was close to being unveiled to the rest of the world.

In June, Michael Hickey returned to Prescott after a sojourn at Hot Springs, Arkansas. He brought back quite a collector's item, which he said would hang over one of the new Hotel Burke's doors and bring good luck to it. It was a horseshoe that had been extricated from General Ulysses S. Grant's horse, Cincinnati. How he came by this acquisition he was reluctant to divulge for fear that the U.S. marshal of Arkansas would pay him a visit.

By June 10, the *Miner* was able to write, "Every day sees another shanty or two torn down and removed from the plaza." June 10 had been the deadline for all temporary businesses to be removed from it, but a few were still waiting for completion of their permanent quarters. They were given some leeway by the city council. The remaining temporary buildings on the plaza were reminders of the terrible July 14 night. Prescottonians were anxious to move on from that memory.

An editorial also ran in the June 10 *Miner* titled "BEAUTIFY THE PLAZA." Because the plaza had been heavily used for almost a year, it was quite beaten up and in disrepair. Reposed in the middle of it, the plaza now looked inconsistent with the new Prescott. The editorial urged, "With the abundant water supply we shall now have, the plaza could be made very beautiful at a small outlay, and those who have benefitted by the use of the plaza should now take an active interest in seeing that the place is made one of beauty and comfort." It was hoped that grass and trees would be planted, with benches in the shade, cement walks and removal of the surrounding fences. The plaza, the editorial stated, should be a reflection of "a real, live, wide awake city as it is, and forbid that it should ever return to look like it did before the fire, more like a cattle corral than a city park."

THE HOTEL BURKE AND PALACE SALOON: GEMS OF THE NEW WHISKEY ROW

The new Hotel Burke was completed, and its grand opening was held on June 12. Its doors swung open at 5:30 p.m. The new hotel had sixty-thousand square feet of floor space, 110 sleeping rooms and 25 rooms for storage and offices. For its time, it was state of the art: "Nothing, in fact that would add to its beauty, convenience or comfort has been overlooked, so that the most wealthy or fastidious may feel all the ease and comfort that they could obtain any place." In the past, commercial travelers would leave for Phoenix to "spend their Sundays and spare time." Now, with the Hotel Burke available and other new and fine modern establishments, it was believed visitors would make it a point to stay in Prescott.

Throughout the Burke was I.X.L. maple flooring, which was "the marvel and admiration of everyone who enters the hotel." The material was renowned not only for its attractiveness but also for its toughness and durability, "being able to wear without splintering or becoming rough for scores of years." Several of the more substantial new buildings also featured the same type of flooring.

Of special beauty was the Hotel Burke's dining room, "as fine a dining room as can be found in the west." It was elegantly furnished and appointed in a manner designed to make it "famous from one end of the country to the other." It could seat 150 people. This room, having held its exquisiteness for more than one hundred years, is still an attraction in today's Hotel St. Michael and is used as a venue for many meetings and events.

The Palace Barbershop was removed from the plaza bandstand on Wednesday, June 26. Brow, Belcher and Smith left their respective temporary quarters on Saturday, June 29. Their new Palace was close to completion.

Hotel Burke became Hotel St. Michael in 1907. *From Norman Fisk.*

Today's Palace Restaurant and Saloon and Hotel St. Michael hearken back to Prescott's 1900–1901 rebuild. *From Norman Fisk.*

The Palace's grand opening was scheduled for the evening of July 3. With the mass of people in town for the Fourth of July celebration, it was bound to be one of the biggest grand openings Prescott had ever seen. In advance of the event, the *Miner* reported, "Only a very brief and incomplete description of such a magnificent building can be given." It also claimed that it was the finest saloon Arizona ever had and "in fact that can be found west of the Mississippi."

The Palace would have made even the most pretentious cities proud. It still does. There is not a more impressive saloon in the West. The first advertisement for the new Palace appeared in the *Miner* on July 16, stating, "New Palace. The most elegant in appointment, most commodious in arrangement and luxurious in equipment of any resort west of the Mississippi and south of the Rockies. It is Just What its name Would imply."

The exterior itself was palatial and ornamental—the interior equally so. Every part of the Palace was the result of the finest workmanship, beginning with massive solid oak doors at the entrance still in use today. Above the doors was frosted plate glass with "Palace" lettered within. Throughout the interior was sawed oak stained in golden color, giving the whole inside an appearance of richness. Upon leaving the main saloon area, the back opened into a seventy-five-foot-wide area that included five private wine rooms and an orchestra stand that would feature some of the best musical talent in Arizona.

The ceiling was steel and finished in gold and copper decorations. It has been repainted since, but the steel is holding up as strong as ever today. Certain sections of the ceiling feature bullet holes of unknown origins.

The most interesting part of the description of the new Palace was that of the bar and the corresponding fixtures. It is intriguing, if not puzzling, that the front bar is described as being brand new, or at least there is that implication. As proven in chapter 10, that same bar was saved during the Great Fire of 1900.

The *Miner* provided a description of both the front and back bars: "The front bar is 24 feet long with departments for four men, and is made of solid oak with polished cherry top and marble base. The back bar is also oak with cherry top and has the finest French plate glass oval top mirrors that are made while the massive columns and carvings to look at with wonder and amazement."

The back bar was a marvel and is still much admired and talked about today. It was a massive piece of Brunswick-Balke-Collender furniture. There have been rumors and reports over the years applied to both the front and

The Palace Saloon's front and back bars shortly after the rebuild in 1901. *From Sharlot Hall Museum.*

back bars. One such rumor is that they were shipped from the East and taken down the Atlantic Ocean around Cape Horn and up the Pacific Ocean before being pulled overland by wagon to Prescott. Another is that they came from San Francisco down the California coastline and up the Colorado River before crossing dry land. However, it is a nearly certain that both the front and back bars simply came by train from San Francisco, where there was a Brunswick-Balke-Collender store. There was no need to first ship either by water to get to their destination.

Not long after their grand reopening, Palace owners began bottling their own whiskey using Cedar Brook as the label. The whiskey was sent in barrels from Lawrenceburg, Kentucky. It was then drawn from the kegs by Palace bartenders and corked in quart-sized bottles.

One report stated that the new Palace was so successful so quickly that within a few months after its opening, Brow, Belcher and Smith offered to pay off the loan that Joseph Mayer had given them. But because the loan had been given with interest, he refused. He had not made this

The Palace Saloon's interior in the early 1900s looks much the same as it does today. *From Sharlot Hall Museum.*

agreement to break even, and he intended to collect the full amount with interest accrued.

Above the saloon was the beautiful Palace Hotel, still being completed on July 4, 1901. Today, it is another of the great saloons of today's West: The Jersey Lilly Saloon. High above the Palace Hotel (and the Jersey Lilly today) was created a beautiful work of art that has mostly gone unnoticed over the decades. It is something special with significant meaning behind it.

As alluded to earlier, pre-fire Palace owner Bob Brow was an avid patriot and ardent supporter of Theodore Roosevelt's Rough Riders during the Spanish-American War. He wanted something to commemorate that time and the sacrifices made by Prescott and Yavapai County men. The *Prospect* provided a description and explanation:

> *On the second floor a deep, open alcove with balustrade of pressed brick and granite trimmings, forms a lofty, roofed balcony extending across the entire front. Corresponding to the spacious portal below, its vaulted ceiling is*

supported by polished shafts of granite on either side, while surmounting the whole, above the capitals of the tall granite columns, a triangular, sunken niche extends across the face of the building in which appears in bas-face a device symbolical of Arizona and her two companies of Territorial troops who so nobly comported themselves during the late war with Spain. In the center is depicted the great seal of Arizona Territory, and rampant on either side are the life-like figures of two animals native to Arizona—a mountain lion and a bear.

On the occasion of the departure to the war of the respective companies of Arizona troops, Bob Brow, an enthusiastic admirer of the "soldier boys," presented to each of them a living specimen of Arizona's best fighting beasts to be their mascots. To the Rough Riders, he gave a mountain lion and to the Volunteers a bear, and each company immediately adopted the new recruit as its mascot and took it with them through all their dangers and adventures.

And while few notice, it stands high above Whiskey Row today.

FOURTH OF JULY IN NEW PRESCOTT

It became important for residents to celebrate the Fourth of July in 1901 and, in so doing, to introduce and celebrate the new Prescott. Plans began well in advance for the three-day festivity. Horse races, steer roping, drilling contests and a fireman's tournament were among the scheduled events. There would be fireworks, a parade, "literary exercises" and a grand ball.

So that Phoenicians could enjoy Prescott's Independence Day celebration, and, for many, to see the new Prescott, a special train left Phoenix at seven in the morning and arrived in Prescott at one o'clock in the afternoon on all three days. By Wednesday, July 3, hotels were overflowing. Those arriving on July 4 had difficulty finding lodging.

Although it was announced that the celebration would take place July 4–6, it actually commenced on July 3, with fireworks orchestrated by the Palace's Barney Smith and lasting until 1:00 a.m. Around that time, "the town seemed to go to sleep, but by 5 o'clock a portion of it was awake again ushering in 'the day we celebrate.'"

On July 4, festivities opened on the courthouse plaza at 9:30 a.m., with a Phoenix band concert that was enjoyed by many. Local schoolchildren sang

"The Star-Spangled Banner." Mrs. Thomas Bates recited the Declaration of Independence, which was followed by oration from the eloquent Senator Eugene Ives, who "showed careful and deep thought and a harmonious grouping of ideas."

From two to five o'clock in the afternoon, competitions involving fireman skills took place. That was followed by a hilarious parade put on by a group of fun-loving men, calling themselves the Horribles, who "with their weird band and grotesque figures, appeared on the streets to the great delight of young America, as well as the amusement of the older ones." The day ended with fireworks.

July 5 was a day of many sporting events. At 9:00 a.m., miners' double-handed and single-handed drilling contests began. First prize for the double-handed competition was $200, while the single-handed winner would collect $100. At the racetrack, cowboys participated in a ten-mile relay race where one rider would use five horses and switch horses every half mile. There were also half-mile races and bronco riding.

The plaza featured eleven events for boys only. There were fifty- and one hundred–yard footraces; potato races, where ten potatoes were moved from one place to another; sack and three-legged races; and a bicycle race around the perimeter of the plaza. There was even a burro race around the plaza. The winner received two dollars. That was a lot of money for a youngster then, almost sixty dollars for a burro-riding boy today.

The night ended with a masquerade ball put on by the Elks Club. The *Prospect* observed on July 6, "Prescott was the liveliest town in the southwest this week, her crowded streets reminded us all of old times." On July 5, a gun shooting tournament and rodeo events organized by George Ruffner took place. The rodeo allowed women to participate in a half-mile saddle horse race. The first-place prize was a "fancy bridle valued at $40." The biggest event was the steer-tying contest, which was "open to the world."

The greatest sensation during the three-day celebration was created by Hazel Keyes, a world-renowned aeronaut, who made parachute jumps every evening from a Prescott-made hot air balloon. The ascension of the balloon bore a metaphorical connotation to Prescott folks, because it would be "emblematic of the way the town 'went up' in smoke."

Keyes's personal balloon was sixty feet long, but for the jumps she would need a bigger balloon. It was the largest ever used in Arizona up to that point—eighty feet long and requiring eight hundred yards of muslin to construct it. Three sewing machines were employed during the days before

Keyes's jumps, and some of the sewing was done by the aeronaut herself. The furnace to supply the balloon with hot air was constructed on the southeast corner of the plaza. She invited newspapermen to fly with her in her balloon during a test flight, but to a man they rejected the invitation. Instead, they nominated Bob Brow's pets—a raccoon and a trick monkey.

On the Fourth, the departure for the first ascension was scheduled for 7:00 p.m. But it took more time to fill the big balloon than anticipated: "The monster airship swayed to and fro as it was being filled, tugging at the ropes as though anxious to get away." Twenty men held the balloon down. When it was filled to about 75 percent of its capacity, Keyes strapped herself onto the balloon's trapeze, and at about 7:40 p.m., she shouted to the men, "Good bye all; let her go!"

The balloon was freed from its moorings. One of the ropes broke, and it was feared an accident would result, but the balloon righted itself. It quickly rose in a northeasterly direction to heights between three thousand and four thousand feet, "when the daring aeronaut looked no larger than a bird suspended in mid air." Three men followed her flight path by horseback. After the balloon passed over the Citizen's Cemetery between Gurley and Sheldon streets, Keyes cut herself from the trapeze, and her parachute soon gracefully opened.

At first, the descent was slow. But because the aeronaut had preselected a site for her lighting, she was forced to sway the parachute from side to side to accelerate the descent. She came down about a mile and a half east of town, landing in a cluster of bushes and scratching her face a bit. No other injuries were sustained. The parachute dragged Miss Keyes a few feet before it came to a stop.

The men who had followed her on horseback were there to help just after she landed. Other than to free her from the parachute, she needed no help. Fearing it was damaged, Keyes asked the men about the condition of her balloon. Freed from its human cargo, the balloon had swayed to and fro for some time and finally careened about a half mile from Keyes before rolling into a big ball of muslin.

The next night's ascension rendered a mishap. The balloon was unable to reach the heights it had achieved the night before. After takeoff, a stream of carriages and horseback riders followed Keyes's flight path. This time the balloon headed east toward Pleasant Street, four blocks away, where Keyes cut the rope from the balloon. She allowed herself to drop rapidly for about 150 feet before freeing the parachute.

Barely seven minutes after the balloon was released from its bond with gravity, the parachutist landed hard, severely spraining both ankles. She was placed in a carriage and rushed to Dr. McNally, who treated her. The balloon once again landed just east of Citizen's Cemetery.

Going against the advice of friends, Keyes would not allow her injuries to prevent her from fulfilling her promise to make three jumps while in Prescott, which rendered her much admiration: "That she thoroughly understands her business she has certainly demonstrated, and she has also demonstrated that a flight through the air and a daring leap of 3000 feet has no more terror for her than a promenade on the streets," praised the *Miner*.

When the evening of Saturday, July 6, spun around there was less wind than the previous night, and Keyes was once more ready to strap herself to her balloon. It was filled more fully than the times before, which enabled it to reach and sustain the height of four thousand feet. Because of the milder winds, it traveled more slowly eastward. When near the eastern limits, Keyes set herself free from the balloon.

Her descent this time went "slowly and gracefully." The balloon, however, not so much. It did a sudden somersault, turning upside down, which forced the air from the balloon to exit and produce propulsion. It sped to the ground "like a tumbler pigeon," then crashed and rolled into a ball. About the same time, Miss Keyes alit more northward than the previous jumps, just southwest of Fort Whipple in open land free of brush and about one hundred yards from her balloon. She landed smoothly and avoided further injury to her ankles.

Returning to Prescott, Keyes was greeted by a large crowd in front of the Hotel Burke. She was thanked for her part in making this Fourth of July celebration even more exciting and memorable. In return, and much to the delight of those present, the aeronaut announced that she would be moving to Prescott to take up permanent residence.

And why would she not? The thirty-seven-year-old Prescott was now a brand-new modern town. It held more promise than ever. A proverbial page of history had been turned, and another book about the pearl of the Central Arizona Highlands was waiting to be written.

EPILOGUE

The great fire of 1900 was the best thing that ever happened to Prescott.
—Morris Goldwater

Whiskey Row's post–Great Fire history and stories, dear reader, shall be shared another day. But for now, it is hoped that it is clear that Prescott had crossed its Rubicon. The New Prescott caught the attention of outsiders from the East and the West, the North and South. They marveled at how such a modern and attractive town could be built in such a short time.

Many Prescottonians believed that their new town was now on the map, that before the Great Fire it was a little-known village. Locals were no longer calling their place of residence a town, but a city.

Even though it was the most destructive urban fire Prescott, and perhaps even Arizona, would ever know, the tragedy led to Prescott's most constructive phase. The Great Fire proved to be Prescott's great oxymoron—a constructive destruction. More than a few people believed it was the best thing to ever happen to Prescott. Businesses—some of which were described as clapboard shacks, especially along Whiskey Row—were rebuilt into more aesthetically satisfying, stronger, fire-resistant structures. The new had come, and the old was wiped clean.

Prescottonian Francis Veile spoke of the result of the Whiskey Row Fire of 1900: "Just as it takes furnace heat to fuse the metals to make good steel, so did the great fire burn out the dross and weld Prescott into a community of indomitable spirit." Although *dross* may be a harsh word for old Prescott, the sentiment is true.

Future city manager John Robinson said, "Prescott is a bigger and better town because the old Prescott burned in 1900."

William Hardy, the famous pioneer who founded what is now Bullhead City, volunteered for jury duty in Prescott in July 1901 because he wanted to see the reconstructed Prescott. Amazed at what he saw, Hardy claimed it now had "some of the finest buildings on the continent, in fact in the world."

The *Prospect* took a glance back in 1902: "How trivial seem our troubles, after they have passed! That fire, terrible as it was, was a necessary factor in Prescott's advancement to better things. It merely marked the first milestone in her progress; and now she stands facing the new century, strengthened and beautified by the trials she has endured and overcome; gazing with serene confidence into the golden future."

The new Prescott and its Whiskey Row were the talk of the West. Whiskey Row would endure gambling and alcohol prohibitions. It would be the sites for two major motion pictures: *Junior Bonner*, starring Steve McQueen, and the cult classic *Billy Jack*. *Wish Man*, the story of local resident Frank Shankwitz, founder of the Make-A-Wish Foundation, was filmed in Prescott, with perhaps its most important scene taped in the Palace Restaurant and Saloon.

Although Prescott and Whiskey Row went through many changes, unlike so many Old West towns and sites that went bottom up and/or later became tourist attractions, both are alive and kicking today. Prescott is a thriving city with the feel of a small town, and Whiskey Row is both a tourist attraction and business district.

Whiskey Row has been called Arizona's most legendary block. Today, it is visited by people from all over the world. For them, it is a refreshing brush with the past—a bit of a step back in time. But it is more. It is what the West has become and where the West is headed.

However, Whiskey Row proprietors know that if not for the Row's integral link to the Old and Wild West, it is just another row of shops and one might as well visit a strip mall in Phoenix.

BIBLIOGRAPHY

Books

Author unknown. *The Great Prescott Fire of July 14, 1900: Centennial Commemoration, July 14–16, 2000*. Prescott, AZ: City of Prescott, 2000.

Chaput, Don. *Virgil Earp: Western Peace Offer*. Encampment, WY: Affiliated Writers of America, 1994.

Collins, Jan Mackell. *Wicked Women of Prescott, Arizona*. Charleston, SC: The History Press, 2013.

Courtney, Bradley G. *Prescott's Original Whiskey Row*. Charleston, SC: The History Press, 2015.

Jackson, Eric Conrad. *Prescott's Fire Department*. Charleston, SC: Arcadia Publishing, 2014.

Savage, Pat. *One Last Frontier: A Story of Indians, Early Settlers, and the Old Ranches of Northern Arizona*. New York: Exposition Press, 1964.

Journals

Bates, Al. "Arizona Escapes from New Mexico." *Territorial Times* 7, no. 2 (May 2014): 4–5.

———. "An Embarrassing Start to a Long Journey West." *Territorial Times* 7, no. 2 (May 2014): 10–21.

———. "General James Carleton Gets Involved." *Territorial Times* 7, no. 2 (May 2014): 7–9.

———. "Gold Is Discovered in the Central Arizona Highlands." *Territorial Times* 7, no. 2 (May 2014): 5–7.

———. "The New Officials Take Charge." *Territorial Times* 7, no. 2 (May 2014): 22–28.

———. "Prescott Celebrates the Fourth of July." *Territorial Times* 7, no. 2 (May 2014): 29.

———. "President Polk Creates the American Southwest." *Territorial Times* 7, no. 2 (May 2014): 1–3.

Collins, Thomas P. "Dan Thorne: A Whiskey Row Success Story." *Territorial Times* 4, no. 2 (May 2011): 16–22.

Goldberg, Isaac. "An Old Timer's Experiences in Arizona." Arizona Historical Review 2, no. 3 (October 1929): 88–94.

Articles

Collins, Tom. "Andrew L. Moeller: Pioneer, Entrepreneur, Philanthropist." Parts I and II. Sharlot Hall Museum Library and Archives. *Dailey Courier* Days Past archives. May 20 and 27, 2010.

———. "Prescott's Famous 'Fireproof' Hotel." Parts I and II. Sharlot Hall Museum Library and Archives. *Dailey Courier* Days Past archives. July 24 and 31, 2010.

Courtney, Brad. "Barry Goldwater's One Regret: 'You Rascal You…'" Sharlot Hall Museum Library and Archives. *Dailey Courier* Days Past archives. September 12, 2012.

———. "Building the Diana: Cornerstone of Early Montezuma Street Saloons." Sharlot Hall Museum Library and Archives. *Dailey Courier* Days Past archives. March 12, 2016.

———. "The Legend of the Quartz Rock Saloon and the Origins of Whiskey Row." Sharlot Hall Museum Library and Archives, *Dailey Courier* Days Past archives. March 1, 2014.

———. "Prelude to Prescott's Great Fire of 1900." Sharlot Hall Museum Library and Archives. *Dailey Courier* Days Past archives. June 17, 2017.

———. "The Three Other Fires that Shaped Whiskey Row." Sharlot Hall Museum Library and Archives. *Dailey Courier* Days Past archives. October 15, 2016.

————. "Whiskey Row's Dynamic 'D.C.' Thorne." Parts I and II. Sharlot Hall Museum Library and Archives. *Dailey Courier* Days Past archives. November 18 and 25, 2017.

————. "Whiskey Row's Virgil Earp." Sharlot Hall Museum Library and Archives. *Dailey Courier* Days Past archives. November 26, 2016.

Newspapers

Arizona Miner
Arizona Republican
Arizona Weekly Journal-Miner
Arizona Weekly Miner
Daily Courier
Howler
Los Angeles Herald
Prescott Weekly Courier
Prospect
Weekly Arizona Miner
Weekly Republican

ABOUT THE AUTHOR

 radley G. Courtney, author of *Prescott's Original Whiskey Row*, is an independent historian who lived and taught in inner-city Phoenix, Arizona, for nineteen years and on the Navajo Indian Reservation in northern Arizona for twelve years. For six of those years, he was also a riverboat pilot and guide who gave tours down the incomparable canyons of the Colorado River. Brad has recorded three albums of original music and has appeared on CNN, the Travel Channel and numerous other television stations across the country. He holds a master's degree in history from California State University. Brad is also the founder of Whiskey Row History Walking Tours.

Visit us at
www.historypress.com